CAMBRIDGE

EMPOWER

SECOND EDITION

WORKBOOK
WITHOUT ANSWERS

B2
UPPER INTERMEDIATE

Wayne Rimmer

CONTENTS

Matt Tony Jessie Alyssia

1A | SHE IS AN INSPIRING WOMAN

1 GRAMMAR Review of tenses

a Underline the correct words to complete the text.

The other day, I was walking down the street when I ¹*have seen / was seeing / saw* Sam Carter, you know, the famous film director. I was really excited because he ²*has been / is / was* one of my favourite directors for ages and I watch his films all the time. 'What ³*is he doing / does he do / has he done* here?' I thought to myself. There was only one way to find out. Sam ⁴*went / was going / has gone* into a café, but I stopped him before he got inside and said, 'Hi, Sam!' He smiled at me and we started to talk outside. Me and Sam Carter! He always ⁵*is looking / looks / has looked* so serious in photos, but he's a really friendly guy. In the end, Sam ⁶*invites / has invited / invited* me for a coffee. Then he told me why he was in town. His film company ⁷*made / has made / were making* a new film and they have lots of new faces in it, just ordinary people, but they need some more.

'How about you?' Sam asked. '⁸*Did you watch / Have you watched / Are you watching* any of my films? Do you want to be in one?' I was so shocked, I ⁹*have dropped / was dropping / dropped* my cup on the floor! The hot coffee went all over Sam; he screamed and ran outside. I lost my big chance!

b ▶ `01.01` Listen and check.

c Complete the sentences with the correct forms of the verbs in the box: present simple, present continuous, present perfect, past simple, past continuous or past perfect.

come	do	not finish	get	not have
meet	produce	remember	~~work~~	write

1 John __is working__ in a small marketing agency at the moment.
2 _____ you ever _____ anybody famous?
3 **A** What _____ you _____?
  B I'm a student.
4 Shakespeare _____ plays and poetry and thousands of words in English come from them.
5 Our friends _____ for dinner, but they had to cancel because they were ill.
6 Not many people _____ her well now.
7 He was rich and famous, but he _____ many friends.
8 The game _____ yet, there are five minutes to go.
9 Things _____ slowly _____ worse in the office now that Mrs Andrews has retired.
10 Eva was very happy with the design samples that Tom _____ .

2 VOCABULARY Character adjectives

a Underline the correct words to complete the sentences.

1 Don't be so *motivated / stubborn / ambitious*! You know what I am saying makes sense.
2 Ethan is very *sensitive / inspiring / passionate*. He gets upset when the teacher corrects him in class.
3 Margarita is a really *inspiring / sensitive / arrogant* woman and an example to everyone.
4 Susan is *motivated / optimistic / passionate* about basketball and trains every day.
5 He's rude and *sensitive / determined / arrogant* – he thinks he's better than everyone else.
6 If you are *motivated / self-confident / pessimistic*, you do things because you really want to do them.

b Complete the crossword puzzle.

→ **Across**
1 showing firm friendship or support
6 not listening to people's opinions or changing your mind
8 thinking about the future in a positive way
↓ **Down**
2 wanting to be successful
3 making a decision and not letting anyone stop you
4 easy to hurt or upset
5 people have a good opinion of you
7 having no experience and expecting things to be all right

3 PRONUNCIATION Sound and spelling: *e*

a How is the underlined letter *e* pronounced in each word in the box? Complete the table with the words.

~~concerned~~ desert desire dessert helpful identity
prefer prizes revise sensitive service slept

Sound 1 /ɪ/ (e.g., *determined*)	Sound 2 /e/ (e.g., *respected*)	Sound 3 /ɜː/ (e.g., *serve*)
		concerned

b ▶ `01.02` Listen and check.

1B | ARE YOU FINDING IT DIFFICULT?

1 GRAMMAR Questions

a <u>Underline</u> the correct words to complete the conversation.

FABIO Hi, there. [1]*You have / Have you got* five minutes?

GABRIELLA Sure. [2]*What / What did* you want to talk to me about?

FABIO Well, I'm doing a triathlon next month. [3]*Didn't / Weren't* you read my post?

GABRIELLA No, I haven't seen it. A triathlon, wow! [4]*What for? / For what?* It sounds really tough!

FABIO It's not easy, yeah, swimming, cycling, then running.

GABRIELLA [5]*What / Which* of those is the most difficult?

FABIO All of them! Er, [6]*weren't / didn't* you a good swimmer once?

GABRIELLA Yeah, once. What are you looking at me like [7]*that for / for that*?

FABIO Do you think [8]*could you / you could* coach me?

GABRIELLA I don't know [9]*whether / what* I've got enough time. [10]*Can / Shall* I think about it and phone you later?

FABIO No problem. That's great! I'll swim a lot faster with your help.

GABRIELLA Who [11]*knows / does know*? You might win!

b ▶ 01.03 Listen and check.

c Put the words in the correct order to make questions.

1 a / want / do / marathon / to / you / run ?
   <u>Do you want to run a marathon?</u>

2 to / this / going / is / do / why / she ?
   _____

3 the / register / who / competition / need to / for / doesn't ?
   _____

4 giving / why / our / aren't / tickets / they / us ?
   _____

5 of / which / to do / would you / the challenges / like ?
   _____

6 have / the most / ever done / you / difficult / what is / thing ?
   _____

7 for / did / hard training / what / this / we do / all ?
   _____

8 the / happened / of / what / at / end / the game ?
   _____

9 have / think we / of / a chance / you / do / winning ?
   _____

10 your / who / website / designed ?
   _____

2 VOCABULARY Trying and succeeding

a Complete the sentences with the phrases in the box. There is one extra phrase you do not need.

drop out   give up   keep to   keep it up
manage to   try out   ~~make an effort~~

1 Sandra decided to <u>make an effort</u> to go to the gym every day.

2 José wants to _____ a new recipe for lemon cake.

3 We really need to _____ fast food.

4 Charlie told his kids to _____.

5 The Smiths didn't _____ assemble their kitchen table.

6 It won't be easy to _____ this diet.

b Complete the sentences with the phrases in the box.

give up   ~~have a go~~   keep to   keep it up
make an effort   manage to   drop out   try out   work out

1 I'd like to <u>have a go</u> at snowboarding, but I'm afraid of falling and breaking something.

2 If you _____ of the course, you won't be able to work in your dream job.

3 If you _____ this training programme, you'll get back in shape.

4 Laura applied for a new job, but it didn't _____. She didn't have the right qualifications.

5 My car is in the garage and I don't know if they'll _____ repair it by Monday.

6 Ben went sailing with me twice and he's terrible at it, but he doesn't want to _____.

7 Your writing has improved a lot this term, so _____.

8 Would you like to _____ the new version of the software?

9 I know Jade isn't interested in the project, but she could at least _____ to get involved.

1C EVERYDAY ENGLISH
Don't touch the food!

1 CONVERSATION SKILLS
Breaking off a conversation

a Tick (✓) the best way to break off the conversation.

1 Sorry, but _____ now.
  a ✓ I really must go
  b ☐ I have to finish
  c ☐ there's nothing else to say

2 _____ Speak to you soon.
  a ☐ I've got nothing else to say.
  b ☐ Are we finished?
  c ☐ Got to go.

3 OK, _____.
  a ☐ I look forward to speaking to you
  b ☐ see you tomorrow
  c ☐ that's enough

4 _____, Irena.
  a ☐ Talk to you later
  b ☐ Tell me again
  c ☐ We'll speak about this

5 _____. Can you phone later?
  a ☐ This is not convenient.
  b ☐ Who's speaking?
  c ☐ Can't talk just now.

6 Well, I must _____.
  a ☐ leave
  b ☐ run
  c ☐ end

7 Bye, nice _____.
  a ☐ conversation
  b ☐ talking to you
  c ☐ day

8 Must be _____ now, but thanks for calling.
  a ☐ away
  b ☐ there
  c ☐ off

2 USEFUL LANGUAGE
Explaining and checking understanding

a Put the excerpts in the correct order to explain how to take a good photo.

☐ Always remember to keep still. If the camera moves about, you get a bad photo.

☐ Is that clear? Do you want me to explain any of this again?

☐ But whatever camera you buy, read the instructions carefully. Make sure you know what your camera can do. Have you got that?

☒ 1 You don't need to get a very expensive camera. These have a lot of functions you just don't need. Do you understand what I mean?

☐ Another thing to remember is to take your time. Only real professionals can take good photos in a hurry.

☐ When you take a photo, the most important thing is the light. Basically, the more light, the better, so choose the right time of the day and place. Do you get the idea?

b ▶ 01.04 Listen and check.

3 PRONUNCIATION Rapid speech

a ▶ 01.05 Listen. Tick (✓) the sentences where you hear the final /t/ of the underlined words.

1 ☐ I must go and see her soon.
2 ☐ The nurse said I must eat less bread.
3 ☐ We've got to have more help.
4 ☐ Sorry, you can't take one with you.
5 ☐ Haven't any of the people arrived?
6 ☐ Sarah said she didn't do the homework.
7 ☐ Claudia has been there, hasn't she?
8 ☐ The shop might open again.
9 ☐ We can't use our phones here.
10 ☐ Children mustn't play ball games.

1D SKILLS FOR WRITING
I really missed my phone all day

1 READING

a Read the article. Are the sentences true or false?

1 The woman has the same opinion as most other people.
2 She has noticed an imbalance in communication.
3 The experiment involved the couple not communicating for a day.
4 It was a positive experience for them.
5 Technology has made us forget our priorities.
6 We don't need technology.

b Read the article again and tick (✓) the best ending for the sentences.

1 The purpose of the first paragraph is … .
   a ✓ to explain the writer's motivation
   b ☐ to compare different types of communication
   c ☐ to introduce a theory about communication

2 The main rule of the experiment was that they … .
   a ☐ had to communicate as little as possible
   b ☐ couldn't say anything to each other
   c ☐ needed to explain things very simply

3 The point about breakfast is that … .
   a ☐ making meals involves technology
   b ☐ it was an amusing situation
   c ☐ everything was so simple

4 The rest of the day showed that the experiment … .
   a ☐ needed to continue for longer
   b ☐ only worked until a friend got involved
   c ☐ was not as easy as they thought

5 She texted her husband to discuss … .
   a ☐ plans for a party
   b ☐ the effectiveness of the experiment
   c ☐ her friend's communication problems

6 The conclusion is that … .
   a ☐ the experiment was mostly a failure
   b ☐ technology has changed relationships between people
   c ☐ speaking is still an effective kind of communication

2 WRITING SKILLS
Organising an article

a Read the tips (1–8) for writing an article.
Is the advice good or bad? Tick (✓) the correct box.

When you're writing an article …	Good	Bad
1 plan the structure of your article before you start writing it.	✓	
2 write the article in your own language first, then translate it.		
3 write short paragraphs with one or two sentences.		
4 include questions to engage the reader.		
5 use a dictionary to find interesting words and phrases.		
6 use linking words and expressions to join ideas.		
7 evaluate ideas – write what you think about them.		
8 check your writing when you have finished.		

Face-to-face texting

A lot of people think that technology brings people closer together, but I'm not so sure. People spend so much time texting and looking at screens that they hardly ever speak to one another. This made me think, and I decided to do a little experiment.

One day my husband and I decided not to speak to each other at all. We could email, text, etc., but we couldn't actually communicate in spoken words. So, at breakfast, he sent me a text to ask if I wanted any more toast and I replied that I didn't, but I wouldn't mind another cup of tea.

We both thought it was funny at first, but things got more complicated as the day went on. For example, a friend phoned me about a special party she was organising. I had to text my husband for about 20 minutes to discuss everything.

The whole thing made me appreciate that nothing can replace face-to-face communication – talking to each other. Communication may be easier because of technology, but people aren't machines. We sometimes forget that simple things are often the most important in life.

3 WRITING

a Imagine that for one week you had to walk or cycle to get around rather than use a car or public transport. Write an article about your experience. Use the notes and your own ideas to help you.

Introduction: how you usually get around, your feelings about walking / cycling vs. cars / public transport

Your experience: good things (exercise, see interesting things, cheaper)

Your experience: difficulties (takes longer, bad weather, dangerous?)

Evaluation: walking / cycling better in some situations, should use cars / public transport less

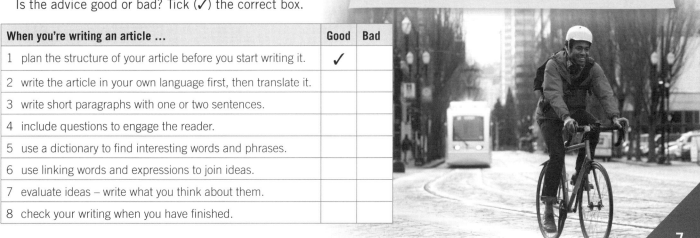

1 READING

a Read the article and tick (✓) the statement that matches Nick's attitude about his own body.

1 ☐ It's more difficult living without arms and legs now than when he was younger.

2 ☐ His physical condition means he is generally worried about trying new things.

3 ☐ He gets on with his life, even though he has no arms or legs.

b Read the article again and tick (✓) the correct answers.

1 Nick's parents knew he would be born without arms and legs.
   a ☐ true   b ☑ false   c ☐ doesn't say

2 Nick was sometimes unhappy when he was at school.
   a ☐ true   b ☐ false   c ☐ doesn't say

3 Nick could swim when he was just 18 months old.
   a ☐ true   b ☐ false   c ☐ doesn't say

4 Nick uses a mouse to operate a computer.
   a ☐ true   b ☐ false   c ☐ doesn't say

5 Nick uses the toe on his foot to play a sport.
   a ☐ true   b ☐ false   c ☐ doesn't say

6 The stadiums where Nick speaks are full.
   a ☐ true   b ☐ false   c ☐ doesn't say

c Write a paragraph about an outstanding person you know or have heard about who has helped others. Remember to include:

• what the person does and why you are impressed by this
• any difficulties the person has had in their life
• how the person has helped other people.

Have you ever thought about what it might be like to live just a single day without being able to use your hands or legs? This is everyday life for Nick Vujicic, who was born without any limbs. However, Nick doesn't let his condition stop him – he regularly takes part in sports, he has travelled all over the world and he's also happily married with a young child. And unlike many able-bodied people, he can even swim and surf.

Before Nick Vujicic was born, his parents had no idea that he would go on to have any medical problems – none of the medical checks had shown a problem. However, when he was born, it was clear that his life would be different from that of other babies. Growing up would not be easy. His parents decided to send him to a neighbourhood school, where he would use a wheelchair and where there were people available to assist him. The experience was difficult, but Nick feels it was the best decision his parents could have made because it gave him a sense of independence. Unsurprisingly, when he was at school, he sometimes felt depressed and lonely and was sometimes bullied. But he always had the support of his loyal friends and family, and these people made him determined to overcome many problems. He even went on to study at university, where he earned a degree in financial planning and real estate.

What surprises many people is just how optimistic Nick can be and how many different things he has managed to do. Much of this is down to his parents. His father put him in the water for the first time when he was 18 months old so that Nick would be self-confident enough to swim when he was older. He has one small foot which he can use to help him move around in the water. He is able to operate a computer by using the toe on this foot to type, something he learned to do when he was just six years old. And when he plays golf – yes, he even plays golf – he is able to hold the golf club under his chin.

A big part of Nick's life now is giving motivational talks. He travels around the world and has shared his inspiring story with millions of people, speaking to audiences in packed stadiums. Nick's message is that you should never give up and that people should love themselves even when they fail.

2 LISTENING

a ▶ 01.06 Listen to Michael and Sarah talking about Frane Selak, who some people have called the unluckiest man in the world. Put the events in the order they happened.

- [ ] a plane crash
- [ ] a bus crash
- [ ] winning the lottery
- [1] a train crash
- [ ] a car accident
- [ ] being hit by a bus
- [ ] a car falling off a mountain

b Listen again and tick (✓) the correct answers.

1 What happened to Selak when he was in the train crash?
   - a [ ] He was very seriously injured.
   - b [✓] He had an injury.
   - c [ ] He wasn't injured.

2 What is true about the plane crash that Selak survived?
   - a [ ] Several other people also survived the crash.
   - b [ ] He escaped through a door after it crashed.
   - c [ ] He was helped by a problem with the plane.

3 What was the cause of the bus crash?
   - a [ ] the weather
   - b [ ] the speed of the bus
   - c [ ] a technical problem with the bus

4 What is true about the first incident with a car that Selak had?
   - a [ ] He was not driving the car when it developed a problem.
   - b [ ] The car exploded just after he got out.
   - c [ ] Flames came into the car from the engine while he was driving it.

5 Why did his car go off the side of the mountain in the later accident?
   - a [ ] He was hit by a lorry.
   - b [ ] He hit a tree and lost control.
   - c [ ] He had to change direction to avoid a lorry.

6 Which of the following sentences is true about when Selak won the lottery?
   - a [ ] He often played the lottery at that time.
   - b [ ] He occasionally played the lottery at that time.
   - c [ ] He had never played the lottery before.

7 What is Sarah's opinion of Selak's story?
   - a [ ] She is sure it's true.
   - b [ ] She is not sure if it's true.
   - c [ ] She is sure it's untrue.

8 What does Michael say about Selak?
   - a [ ] He thinks that Selak is probably telling the truth.
   - b [ ] He thinks that Selak is wrong to invent stories.
   - c [ ] He thinks it's strange that Selak gave away his lottery winnings.

c Write about a time when you were very lucky or unlucky. Use these questions to help you:

- What was the situation? What were you doing?
- Why were you lucky or unlucky?
- How did you feel?
- Was anybody else with you? How did he or she feel?
- Do you think this happens to a lot of people?

⦿ Review and extension

1 GRAMMAR

Tick (✓) the correct sentences. Correct the wrong sentences.

1 [ ] I write this letter to complain about the service.
   I am writing this letter to complain about the service.
2 [ ] Take any train. They all go there.
3 [ ] She lived in that town since she was a child.
4 [ ] Have you ever heard from her again afterwards?
5 [ ] I was having a shower when the water turned cold.
6 [ ] I don't know Tom. How is he?
7 [ ] Why you didn't tell me?
8 [ ] What is the currency in Thailand?

2 VOCABULARY

Tick (✓) the correct sentences. Correct the wrong sentences.

1 [ ] There are determined subjects everyone should study.
   There are certain subjects everyone should study.
2 [ ] Don't mention it to Laura. She's quite sensible about it.
3 [ ] The mayor is very respective in this town.
4 [ ] The president gave a passionated speech about crime.
5 [ ] I'd love to have a go at diving.
6 [ ] I've got a plan, and I'm going to keep to it.

3 WORDPOWER *make*

Match sentences 1–7 with responses a–g.

1 [a] Shall we go by car or walk?
2 [ ] Why is it taking him such a long time to decide?
3 [ ] I'm really afraid of your dog.
4 [ ] Can't you just follow the instructions?
5 [ ] How can I stay in a place like this?
6 [ ] Can you read that sign?
7 [ ] What are the flowers for?

a It makes no difference to me.
b He can never make up his mind.
c It's only trying to make friends.
d Just make the best of it.
e They don't make any sense.
f I want to make up for being late.
g No, I can't make out what it says.

↻ REVIEW YOUR PROGRESS

Look again at Review Your Progress on p. 18 of the Student's Book. How well can you do these things now?
3 = very well   2 = well   1 = not so well

I CAN ...	
discuss people I admire	[ ]
discuss a challenge	[ ]
explain what to do and check understanding	[ ]
write an article.	[ ]

IT WAS GETTING LATE AND I WAS LOST

1 GRAMMAR Narrative tenses

a Underline the correct words to complete the sentences.

1 I *had* / *was having* / *had had* a shower and ran for the bus.
2 Sorry, when you called, I *spoke* / *was speaking* / *had spoken* to a customer.
3 By the time Jane arrived for dinner, everyone *left* / *had left* / *has left*.
4 He *set* / *had set* / *was setting* the watch to 00:00 and began to run the marathon.
5 The phone *had been* / *was* / *has been* ringing for about a minute when I answered it.
6 What *have you done* / *had you done* / *were you doing* in the garage all that time?
7 We *were buying* / *bought* / *had been buying* some fruit and went to the next shop.
8 Someone *had broken* / *was breaking* / *had been breaking* the window, but we didn't see who it was.
9 Hi, *had you waited* / *were you waiting* / *you waited* for me?
10 The manager stood up and *had made* / *was making* / *made* a speech.

b Complete the text with the correct forms of the words in brackets.

> One afternoon some years ago, I ¹ _was thinking_ (think) about what to do when my friend Janice phoned. She was in a good mood because she ² _____ (finish) all her exams.
> She ³ _____ (come) round and we decided to go for a walk in the mountains. We ⁴ _____ (go) very far – only 4,000 steps on my phone app – when the weather suddenly changed. Until that moment, it ⁵ _____ (be) warm and sunny, but the sky very quickly turned dark and it ⁶ _____ (begin) to rain heavily. We ⁷ _____ (take) our coats or umbrellas with us, and we ⁸ _____ (get) very wet. We ⁹ _____ (run) to a nearby tree to take shelter, hoping the rain would soon stop, but ten minutes later the temperature dropped and it ¹⁰ _____ (start) snowing. We walked back the way we ¹¹ _____ (come) earlier, but the small bridge we had crossed before was now under water, as the river had burst its banks. I tried to phone for help, but my battery ¹² _____ (die) and Janice ¹³ _____ (forget) to bring her phone. By then it ¹⁴ _____ (get) dark and we ¹⁵ _____ (be) very scared. Imagine our relief when suddenly we saw the lights of a farmer's truck. He was out looking for a lost sheep – and he rescued us!

c ▶ 02.01 Listen and check.

2 VOCABULARY Expressions with *get*

a Complete the sentences with the words in the box.

attention	away	~~down~~	hold	involved	point	rid	swept

1 All this grey weather is really getting me ____ *down* ____, and I feel quite depressed.
2 There isn't enough space. We need to get _____ of all this rubbish.
3 I tried to get _____ of the balloon, but I couldn't and it floated away.
4 The waves are really big, so be careful not to get _____ away.
5 Let's get straight to the _____ and not waste time.
6 To get the waiter's _____ in this restaurant, you need to ring the bell.
7 It's been a very long term. I'd like to get _____ this summer – not sure where.
8 Don't get _____ in all Karen's problems. People will start blaming you.

b Complete the sentences under the pictures with the expressions in the box.

| get through | ~~get to~~ | get into trouble | get anywhere |
| get the feeling | get on my nerves | | |

1 I had fun with my brother. I hope I'll _get to_ play with him again soon.
2 I'm not sure I'll _____ all this today.
3 I _____ this will be over quickly.
4 The company won't _____ with this new product.
5 He might _____ going to school like that.
6 All this crying is starting to _____.

3 PRONUNCIATION *had been*

a ▶ 02.02 Listen to the sentences and tick (✓) the ones that include *had*.

Sentence 1	✓	Sentence 6	☐
Sentence 2	☐	Sentence 7	☐
Sentence 3	☐	Sentence 8	☐
Sentence 4	☐	Sentence 9	☐
Sentence 5	☐	Sentence 10	☐

2B IF IT RUNS TOWARDS YOU, DON'T RUN AWAY

1 GRAMMAR
Future time clauses and conditionals

a Underline the correct words to complete the conversation.

MARIO Hi, Silvia. Are you coming camping with us?

SILVIA ¹*If / When* you still want me to, sure.

MARIO Great. It should be good fun ²*if / unless* the weather gets bad.

SILVIA ³*As long as / If* we get a couple of days of decent weather, I don't mind. What do I need to take?

MARIO The usual stuff. ⁴*When / If* I get home, I'll text you the list I've made just in case. You don't need to worry about food, though. I've packed enough ⁵*in case / provided* you like pasta. That's the easiest thing to make.

SILVIA Fine. ⁶*If / In case* we run out of pasta, I'll take some tins and rice.

MARIO Good idea. ⁷*If / Provided* you want, bring some cards. We could play at night.

SILVIA I'll do that ⁸*when / provided* I don't forget. Text me tomorrow ⁹*as long as / as soon as* you get up.

MARIO OK. Remember to buy pepper spray because we might see bears.

SILVIA ¹⁰*If / Unless* I see a bear, I'll run all the way home!

b ▶ 02.03 Listen and check.

c Match 1–8 with a–h to make sentences.

1. b Phone your mum
2. ☐ It's perfectly safe
3. ☐ I like to go for a swim
4. ☐ It's ideal for a holiday
5. ☐ Take some sun cream
6. ☐ I'll go on the trip
7. ☐ Don't go
8. ☐ You can go any time

a provided you like somewhere quiet.
b when you get there.
c unless you do something stupid.
d as long as you do.
e provided you tell me first.
f in case you need it.
g if you don't want to.
h if it's really warm.

2 VOCABULARY
Animals and the environment

a Find eight words about animals that match these clues.

1. a set of similar animals or plants
2. a living thing that is not a plant
3. the natural surroundings where we live
4. the place where an animal or plant naturally lives or grows
5. kept safe by laws that prevent people from harming them
6. animals or plants that could disappear without our help
7. uncommon and difficult to find
8. catch and kill animals for food or sport

A	E	N	V	I	R	O	N	M	E	N	T	E	U	L
K	N	C	R	H	B	E	X	U	D	D	O	X	K	E
X	D	T	S	G	T	I	C	U	L	E	T	C	E	L
S	A	D	S	N	P	C	L	N	Y	P	B	E	K	M
U	N	Q	E	T	B	S	R	I	A	R	N	P	Y	J
C	G	L	M	R	A	M	A	O	T	O	T	T	X	K
O	E	X	T	T	S	N	R	O	R	T	A	I	J	Z
C	R	E	A	T	U	R	E	Q	K	E	G	O	S	L
S	E	B	R	I	L	L	I	A	N	C	L	N	H	B
F	D	K	I	H	L	E	D	G	N	T	D	A	P	L
U	F	L	A	U	C	C	N	S	P	E	C	I	E	S
L	P	J	H	N	F	Y	Q	T	D	D	G	A	S	R
B	U	V	J	T	J	Z	Q	K	E	I	B	B	B	C
Y	Z	Z	I	I	R	M	P	H	A	B	I	T	A	T
S	K	T	S	X	A	Z	D	I	J	G	B	W	D	X

b Complete the text with the words in the box.

risk ~~creatures~~ environment extinct
natural hunt survive kill

Look at this photo of a group of lions. This might be a very rare sight in the future. Lions are beautiful ¹ *creatures* , but they are very much at ² _____ in the modern world. The European lion has been ³ _____ for 2,000 years and now lions only ⁴ _____ in India and parts of Africa. People still ⁵ _____ lions and ⁶ _____ them, and our damage to the ⁷ _____ is making it difficult for lions to find places to live and feed. We can help by protecting lions' ⁸ _____ habitat, which is the African savannah and the forests of Gujarat in India.

2C EVERYDAY ENGLISH
What a great shot!

1 CONVERSATION SKILLS
Agreeing using question tags

a Complete the question tags in the conversations with the words in the box.

aren't	could	did	don't	haven't	~~isn't~~	shall	wasn't

MIKE It's a beautiful day!
LUCY It's lovely, [1] _____isn't_____ it? Why don't we go to the beach?
MIKE Yes, let's do that, [2] _____ we?
LUCY We could drive but let's walk. We need the exercise.
MIKE We do, [3] _____ we? I'll get my things.
LUCY Last time you forgot your towel.
MIKE I didn't have it with me, [4] _____ I, so I borrowed yours. Anyway, let's go.
Later ...
LUCY That was great, [5] _____ it? I feel really hungry now.
MIKE Me too. This place looks good.
LUCY Yeah, we've been here before, [6] _____ we? It does really good pizza.
MIKE That's right. Oh, I haven't got my wallet. You couldn't lend me some money, [7] _____ you?
LUCY First a towel, then your wallet. You never remember anything.
MIKE Well, we're friends, [8] _____ we? Let's go inside.

b ▶ 02.04 Listen and check.

2 USEFUL LANGUAGE
Giving compliments and responding

a Tick (✓) the best response for the sentences.

1 You're so good at singing.
   a ✓ Do you think so?
   b ☐ What do you think?
   c ☐ I'm glad you like it.
2 Your hair is amazing!
   a ☐ You're welcome.
   b ☐ I'm glad you like it.
   c ☐ I think so.
3 You really managed to get it just right.
   a ☐ Guess it's not bad.
   b ☐ Yes, I managed it.
   c ☐ Didn't I?
4 The colour is just perfect.
   a ☐ Yes, it is.
   b ☐ It's not bad, is it?
   c ☐ That's right, isn't it?
5 It's so tasty!
   a ☐ It's all right.
   b ☐ Not at all.
   c ☐ That's great.
6 That was a lovely present!
   a ☐ The same to you.
   b ☐ Yes, it was.
   c ☐ I'm glad you like it.

b ▶ 02.05 Listen and check.

3 PRONUNCIATION
Intonation in question tags

a ▶ 02.06 Listen to the intonation in the questions. Is the speaker asking a real question or just checking information? Tick (✓) the correct box.

		Asking a question	Checking information
1	It was a great idea, wasn't it?		✓
2	You don't know where Oxford Street is, do you?		
3	That's obvious, isn't it?		
4	They just didn't understand, did they?		
5	He hasn't finished university yet, has he?		
6	I'm not on the team, am I?		
7	They will be able to do it, won't they?		
8	You've been there before, haven't you?		
9	She's forgotten all about it, hasn't she?		
10	She's not going to agree, is she?		

2D SKILLS FOR WRITING
Make sure you know where you're going

1 READING

a Read the leaflet and <u>underline</u> the best heading for each section.

b Read the leaflet again. Are the sentences true or false?

1 It's easy to find an orienteering club.
2 Everyone should do the same training.
3 You should buy some good shoes.
4 You won't need to buy a map.
5 A fast start is important.
6 You should respect the environment you run through.
7 You only need a compass if you get lost.
8 The main thing is to have fun.

2 WRITING SKILLS
Organising guidelines in a leaflet

a Tick (✓) the best introduction to a leaflet with guidelines about collecting mushrooms.

a ☐ For centuries, people have collected mushrooms all over the world. The purpose of this leaflet is to discuss the reasons why mushroom picking is popular and to provide some experiences of people who decided to follow this tradition.

b ☐ Collecting mushrooms might seem like a strange pastime, but it's very popular in many countries, especially in Eastern Europe. You need to be careful about which mushrooms you pick, but this is a fun way of spending time.

c ☐ Why pick mushrooms? Many people think it is better to buy them from a supermarket, but there are advantages to getting them yourself, provided that you don't pick the wrong ones!

d ☐ One day I was at home when my friend phoned and suggested going out to the forest and picking some mushrooms. At first, I thought it was a crazy idea, but I went anyway and actually enjoyed it. Here is my advice for people who want to do the same.

3 WRITING

a Read the plan for the rest of the leaflet. Then complete the leaflet using these headings and notes.

<u>Preparation</u>
1 When? (autumn, mornings)
2 Where? (forests, near trees)
3 Need warm clothes, good shoes/boots
4 Check weather

<u>In the forest</u>
5 Be careful in forest – animals, accidents
6 Only pick mushrooms you know (go with expert, use the Internet)
7 Don't get lost!
8 Protect environment (litter)

<u>At home</u>
9 Eat or freeze mushrooms
10 Many recipes for mushrooms – soup, pies, etc.

Orienteering is a sport where you follow a route with a map and compass and try to get between the points as quickly as possible.

1 *Preparation / Getting Into the Sport / Advantages of Orienteering*
- Orienteering is usually organised in forests. Just search online to find a club near you.

2 *Training / Dangers of Forests / Running Fast*
- You need to be fit to run around forests. If you're lucky, you might live near a forest, but most people will need to do some running in parks or on roads.
- Unless you are very fit already, start with fast walking and then build up to running.

3 *What You Need / Expenses / Shopping for Orienteering*
- You don't need to spend a lot of money on equipment, but a good pair of shoes is essential.
- You'll get a map at the course and you can borrow a compass as well.

4 *Win! / Be Careful! / On the Day*
- Start slowly and save your energy.
- Don't damage any plants or trees. You are only there for the day, but the forest is there forever.
- You won't get lost provided you use your compass and go in a straight line.
- Enjoy yourself!

1 READING

a Read the article about four animals and tick (✓) the things mentioned in the article.

1. ☐ an animal that lives in a different place from its ancestors
2. ☐ an animal that is becoming more and more widespread
3. ☐ an animal made famous in films
4. ☐ an animal that is now extinct
5. ☐ an animal that is important in many countries
6. ☐ an animal that lives close to a lot of humans

b Read the article again. Match the animals 1–4 with the descriptions a–d.

1. ☐ funnel-web spider
2. ☐ great white shark
3. ☐ Komodo dragon
4. ☐ tiger

a This animal has a special ability that allows it to follow other animals more easily.

b This animal may attack humans if they start living in the same environment.

c This animal has attacked humans by accident.

d This animal is often involved in attacks on younger people.

c Read the article again. Are the sentences true or false?

1. Great white sharks normally don't attack humans for food.
2. Attacks on humans by great white sharks are always fatal.
3. Tigers normally stay away from humans.
4. The total number of tigers is large and growing.
5. The Komodo dragon is larger than many of the animals in the group it belongs to.
6. When hunting, the Komodo dragon generally kills the animal it attacks immediately.
7. Some aspects of the behaviour of the funnel-web spider are different from that of other spiders.
8. A bite from any type of funnel-web spider is equally serious.

d Write a paragraph about a special or unusual animal you know something about, or research one on the Internet. Remember to include:

- where it is found – its natural environment and habitat
- whether it is rare, at risk, protected, endangered or extinct
- how it gets its food
- any strategies it uses to find food, to survive or to get an advantage.

TERRIFYING ANIMALS

The animal kingdom is full of frightening creatures – animals you definitely wouldn't want to see close up, apart from perhaps in a zoo. Here are four very different – but equally terrifying – animals.

THE GREAT WHITE SHARK

Most people have heard of this animal – made famous in the *Jaws* films of the 1970s and 1980s. The great white shark has a reputation for being a killer. Perhaps the reputation is unfair because these animals don't normally hunt humans – elephants kill more people than sharks do. But the problem for water sports lovers is that a person swimming on top of a surfboard can look very similar to a seal – a shark's food of preference. If a great white shark does attack a human, the results are not always deadly – it's believed that sharks don't like the taste of humans.

THE TIGER

The tiger is another animal that's probably familiar to most people, even though very few of us have ever seen one in the wild. Tigers have fascinated us since ancient times and are very important to a number of cultures in Asia – they are the national animal of Bangladesh, India, Vietnam, Malaysia and South Korea. Tigers are the largest of all the cat species; they're fast runners, not to mention excellent swimmers. The good news is that they generally avoid contact with people, although they do attack, particularly when humans start to move into their natural habitats. It should also be added that tigers are now endangered, and humans play a very large role in this.

THE KOMODO DRAGON

The Komodo dragon is a very large lizard – it can grow as long as 3 metres and weigh up to 70 kg. Experts think Komodo dragons are related to ancient lizards from Australia, but they're now found only on some islands in Indonesia. They are probably most famous for their unusual methods of killing. When hunting, they attack but don't kill the other animal right away. This is because they have a poisonous bite, so after attacking the animal, they follow it until it dies from the poison, a job made easier thanks to their excellent sense of smell. While attacks on humans are rare, they can and do happen.

THE FUNNEL-WEB SPIDER

Many people are afraid of spiders, although the vast majority are completely harmless to humans. But there are of course a number of species that can be dangerous, and the funnel-web spider is certainly among them. This spider's natural habitat is in the area around the Australian city of Sydney. It can be between one and five centimetres long, and is dark blue, brown or black. Unlike many other spiders, this species can be quite aggressive when it comes into contact with humans. When it attacks, it holds on tight and can bite several times. A bite from a Sydney funnel-web spider is extremely painful and can kill quickly, although bites from the females are less severe. Children are particularly at risk – 42% of attacks involve children rather than adults.

2 LISTENING

a ▶ 02.07 Listen to a news story and tick (✓) the correct answer.

1 ☐ A woman will probably recover after spending a week in her car.
2 ☐ A woman is currently in hospital after spending more than two weeks in her car.
3 ☐ A woman is very ill after spending over a month in her car.

b Listen again and tick (✓) the correct answers.

1 When Alicia Lone didn't come back shortly after 9 pm, her family … .
  a ☐ felt sure that something bad had happened
  b ✓ were not immediately worried
  c ☐ immediately called the police

2 The police knew … .
  a ☐ what time Lone had left work
  b ☐ the route she had taken home
  c ☐ where she had been planning to go after work

3 The police think she turned off the main road … .
  a ☐ because she had had a problem with her car
  b ☐ because of the weather
  c ☐ to have a break

4 The police say Lone … .
  a ☐ knew she would have to spend a long time in the car
  b ☐ had turned the car round and driven back towards the main road
  c ☐ wasn't able to move the car because the weather conditions had got worse

5 The police … .
  a ☐ have got all the details from Lone of what happened
  b ☐ have only been able to speak to Lone for a short period of time
  c ☐ haven't been able to visit the hospital yet

6 The reason nobody had found the car earlier was that … .
  a ☐ few cars drive in that area at that time of year
  b ☐ there was maintenance work, so no cars could reach the area
  c ☐ the car was totally covered in snow

7 The reason Lone survived might be that … .
  a ☐ she had a lot of food with her in the car
  b ☐ she doesn't normally eat or drink much, so it was easier to adapt
  c ☐ her body made a change to deal with the situation she was in

c Write a conversation between two people discussing experiences of very bad weather conditions. Use these questions to help you:

- What kind of weather was it?
- Was the bad weather expected or was it a surprise?
- What kinds of problems did it cause?
- How did they deal with the problems?

⊙ Review and extension

1 GRAMMAR

Tick (✓) the correct sentences. Correct the wrong sentences.

1 ☐ It's been a great week. On Tuesday, I have met an old friend.
  It's been a great week. On Tuesday, I met an old friend.
2 ☐ In those days, people spent more time outside.
3 ☐ I met Sarah three years ago, when I had been a student.
4 ☐ She has been waiting for a chance and finally she got one.
5 ☐ Lucy had been seeing Michael for some time.
6 ☐ I'll watch it in case it's on TV.

2 VOCABULARY

Tick (✓) the correct sentences. Correct the wrong sentences.

1 ☐ The fish was too slippery for me to hold and it get away.
  The fish was too slippery for me to hold and it got away.
2 ☐ I can't get over how big that tiger is.
3 ☐ I'm sorry, I got carried away and lost my temper.
4 ☐ People could do more to protect the enviroment.
5 ☐ Every year, hundreds of animal races just disappear.
6 ☐ The Siberian tiger could soon become extinguished.

3 WORDPOWER *face*

Complete the sentences with the expressions in the box.

can't face   face a difficult choice   ~~face fell~~
face the fact   face the music   say it to my face

1 Carmel really wanted the dress, but her ___*face fell*___ when she saw how expensive it was.
2 I have to _____ that I'm not as young as I used to be.
3 John is so hypocritical. If he's unhappy with what I did, he should _____.
4 I _____ going to work today. I need a day off.
5 Is it better to get a job or go to university? Young people _____ nowadays.
6 My wife will be really angry, but I'm going to have to tell her the truth and _____.

⟳ REVIEW YOUR PROGRESS

Look again at Review Your Progress on p. 30 of the Student's Book. How well can you do these things now?
3 = very well   2 = well   1 = not so well

I CAN ...	
discuss dangerous situations	☐
give advice on avoiding danger	☐
give and respond to compliments	☐
write guidelines in a leaflet.	☐

3A | I'M NOT VERY GOOD IN THE MORNING

1 GRAMMAR Multi-word verbs

a Underline the correct words to complete the text.

When I was at school, I didn't think I was good at anything. The other kids picked things ¹*out / in / up* really quickly but I didn't, and I thought some kids looked ²*down on / on down / down* me as some kind of loser. The only thing that interested me was cars and I spent ages in the garage with my mum's old car, looking ³*into / out of / over* how it worked. My mum wasn't ⁴*at / by / into* cars at all, though, and she was tired of me going ⁵*in with / on about / with* them all the time. Anyway, one day there was a school trip. I woke ⁶*by / up / on* early to catch the coach. We were going down the road when the coach suddenly stopped. I thought we had run out ⁷*in / at / of* petrol, but the driver told us there was an engine problem and he would have to call the garage. I went to see for myself and quickly figured ⁸*out / by / through* what to do: I just needed to put back a cable. After ten minutes, the coach was on the road again. After that, everyone looked ⁹*to me up / up to me / me up to,* and I realised there was something I could do well. When I left school, I set ¹⁰*out / up / by* my own car repair business and now I'm doing really well.

b ▶ 03.01 Listen and check.

c Put the words in the correct order to make sentences and questions.

1 all / but / I / threw / sorry, / it / away .
   Sorry, but I threw it all away.

2 let / try / hardest and / your / us / down / don't .
   _____

3 fallen / not friends / out / I've / and we're / Tony / with .
   _____

4 away / you / like that / can't / get / mistakes / with .
   _____

5 yourself / for / it / and figure / go / out .
   _____

6 just / why / don't / it / you / out / try ?
   _____

7 made / Michelle / up / him / it / impress / to .
   _____

8 in / you / you're doing / what / to / believe / need .
   _____

9 up / anyone / a better / come / can / with / idea ?
   _____

10 picked / difficult, / I soon / it / but / is / French / up .
   _____

2 VOCABULARY Ability and achievement

a Underline the correct words to complete the conversation.

MARIANA Have you heard of this writer Daniel Kalder?

LIAM Yes, I read *Strange Telescopes* some time ago. It's a ¹*talented / brilliant* book.

MARIANA I agree. Kalder has got this ²*ability / potential* to make a serious statement but make you laugh at the same time.

LIAM It really is ³*able / outstanding*. I just wish I had some ⁴*ability / talent* for writing.

MARIANA Kalder is ⁵*successful / talented* because he's spent so many years improving his style. That kind of hard work is ⁶*successful / exceptional*.

LIAM True. I don't think many people have heard of Kalder yet, but he has the ⁷*potential / achievement* to be a really well-known writer.

MARIANA He is very ⁸*skilled / potential* at what he does, so good luck to him.

b ▶ 03.02 Listen and check.

c Correct the mistake in each sentence.

1 You need to have a talent to it.
   You need to have a talent for it.

2 Olympic athletes are all exceptional for their field.
   _____

3 She's really successful by what she does.
   _____

4 I became very skilled for the game.
   _____

5 The ability of running long distances is important.
   _____

6 Lesley is brilliant on most ball sports.
   _____

7 He has the potential of being world champion one day.
   _____

8 Carl Lewis was outstanding for the long jump.
   _____

3B | THERE ARE A LOT OF GOOD RUNNERS IN KENYA

1 GRAMMAR
Present perfect and present perfect continuous

a Underline the correct words to complete the sentences and questions.

1 *I've always loved* / *I always loved* rugby. It's my favourite sport.
2 *They've won* / *They won* the championship two years ago.
3 What *have you thought* / *did you think* of the match?
4 The players *haven't arrived* / *didn't arrive* yet, so the match can't begin.
5 *I've been running* / *I was running* in the park when it happened.
6 Marina *has been doing* / *was doing* yoga since she was a teenager.
7 I have *completed* / *been completing* five marathons.
8 **A** Why is your shirt wet?
   B *I've run* / *I've been running*.
9 Joshua hasn't *played* / *been playing* tennis since he was at school.
10 Our judo trainer has *learned* / *been learning* Japanese for ten years.

b Complete the text with the correct forms of the verbs in brackets.

Shantelle Gaston-Hill ¹ <u>has just broken</u> (just / break) a world record! Yesterday in Manchester, England, she ² _____ (run) a half-marathon – that's just over 21 kilometres – in 2 hours, 16 minutes and 3 seconds. And she did it backwards! Shantelle is 32 years old and this is the second time she ³ _____ (beat) all the best runners in the world. From March 2017 to January 2019, Shantelle ⁴ _____ (hold) the world record and now, just ten months later, she ⁵ _____ (set) a new world record!

Shantelle started retro-running – running backwards – for fun, but soon after, she began to take her hobby more seriously. But that's not all! She ⁶ _____ (also / complete) five marathons and eight ultra-marathons. It's safe to say that Shantelle ⁷ _____ (run) forwards and backwards for quite a while!

Every time she ⁸ _____ (race), she ⁹ _____ (represent) a charity. This time Shantelle represented YoungMinds, a mental health charity for children and young people. She wants to show people that consistent training and determination can get extraordinary results.

c ▶ 03.03 Listen and check.

2 VOCABULARY
Words connected with sport

a Read the definitions and write the words.

1 the act of winning a competition _____victory_____
2 a person who is in charge of a sports game _____
3 shout approval or encouragement _____
4 people who watch a sports event _____
5 be in a competition for your country _____
6 an area for playing sport, especially football _____

b Complete the text with the correct forms of the words in brackets.

Everyone thinks that ¹ <u>professional</u> (profession) sportspeople get paid a lot of money to ² _____ (competitor), but this is not always true. The top ³ _____ (athletics) in smaller sports like handball, mountain running and women's cricket don't earn much money. Such sports are very ⁴ _____ (competition) and the athletes ⁵ _____ (training) hard, but even if they ⁶ _____ (representation) their country, they often can't make a living from their sport. Unfortunately, ⁷ _____ (victor) in ⁸ _____ (champion) and new world ⁹ _____ (recording) very often don't mean money, especially if the sport isn't popular on TV. But maybe this doesn't matter if the athletes enjoy what they do and spectators are happy to watch them perform and ¹⁰ _____ (cheerful) for them. Money isn't everything, after all.

c ▶ 03.04 Listen and check.

3 PRONUNCIATION Word stress

a ▶ 03.05 Listen to the conversation and underline the stressed syllables in the highlighted words.

ELENA I know you like ¹athletics, but do you ever take part in ²competitions?

DIMA Sometimes – in fact, I'm going to ³compete in the national ⁴championships next weekend.

ELENA So you're almost a ⁵professional ⁶athlete then?

DIMA Not really. It's hardly a ⁷profession but I do a lot of ⁸training, and I'm hoping for a good ⁹performance. There'll be a lot of strong ¹⁰competitors and I'll have to ¹¹perform really well on the day.

ELENA So ¹²victory might be yours then, and we'll welcome the ¹³victorious champion home?

DIMA Don't laugh, I might win!

1 USEFUL LANGUAGE Making careful suggestions; Keeping to the topic of the conversation

a Put the words in the correct order to make statements and questions.

1 could / go / swimming / we / day / always / another .
   We could always go swimming another day.

2 thing / price / remember / another / to / is the .
   _____

3 stay / maybe / I / should / home / think / we .
   _____

4 idea / ask / think / to / a / don't you / it's / good ?
   _____

5 how / sound / we watch / does / on Sunday / a / film / if / it ?
   _____

6 to / that / but / easier / it'd / eat out / agree / be / don't you ?
   _____

b Correct the mistake in each sentence.

1 Don't you think it's a good idea take some food?
   Don't you think it's a good idea to take some food?

2 Anyway, as I was speaking, Tessa needs to decide.
   _____

3 Another idea might be for going the day before.
   _____

4 Just going to what I was saying before.
   _____

5 I thought maybe we could to invite Simon.
   _____

6 Of course, we could always checking online.
   _____

7 But don't you agree that it's be better to ask first?
   _____

8 So, to get back at Martin and his problems.
   _____

2 PRONUNCIATION Consonant sounds

a Decide if the underlined letters have a voiced sound or unvoiced sound. Write *V* (voiced) or *U* (unvoiced).

1 <u>g</u>ame [V]   <u>c</u>ame [U]   6 sa<u>v</u>e [ ]   sa<u>f</u>e [ ]
2 <u>b</u>each [ ] <u>p</u>each [ ]   7 <u>p</u>ie [ ]   <u>b</u>uy [ ]
3 <u>f</u>erry [ ] <u>v</u>ery [ ]   8 <u>p</u>ig [ ]   <u>p</u>ick [ ]
4 <u>s</u>imple [ ] <u>s</u>ymbol [ ] 9 <u>p</u>ack [ ]   <u>b</u>ack [ ]
5 <u>g</u>irl [ ]   <u>c</u>url [ ]   10 ha<u>v</u>e a [ ] ha<u>v</u>e to [ ]

b ▶ 03.06 Listen and check.

3D SKILLS FOR WRITING
It doesn't matter what sport people choose

1 READING

a Look at the bar chart and read the article. Match paragraphs 1–5 with their functions a–e.

- a ☐ It adds extra information not shown in the data.
- b ☐ It interprets the data in more detail.
- c ☐ It states some additional things to consider about the data and the future.
- d ☑ 1 It outlines the issue that the data tries to answer.
- e ☐ It explains what the bar chart is about.

b Look at the bar chart and read the article again. Tick (✓) the correct answers.

1 The chart includes 13-year-olds from Ireland.
  a ☐ true   b ☐ false   c ☑ doesn't say

2 Information about schools is included.
  a ☐ true   b ☐ false   c ☐ doesn't say

3 Older teenagers are walking more.
  a ☐ true   b ☐ false   c ☐ doesn't say

4 There is no great change between the figures for cycling.
  a ☐ true   b ☐ false   c ☐ doesn't say

5 There are no major patterns in the data.
  a ☐ true   b ☐ false   c ☐ doesn't say

6 The article ends with a reference to the future.
  a ☐ true   b ☐ false   c ☐ doesn't say

2 WRITING SKILLS Describing data

a Look at the bar chart below that compares sports fans by generation across different sports in the USA. Then complete the sentences with the numbers and words in the box. There are two extra ones you do not need.

> 16 ~~5~~ 3 20 decrease increase least most

1 Only about ___5___ % of millennials are big fans of soccer.
2 However, the percentage of loyal basketball fans has remained the same at _____ %.
3 The _____ popular sport in the USA is American football.
4 There has been a slight _____ in the percentage of loyal sports fans in most sports.
5 There has been about a _____ % drop in hockey fans from the previous generation.
6 About _____ % of Generation X closely watch baseball in the USA.

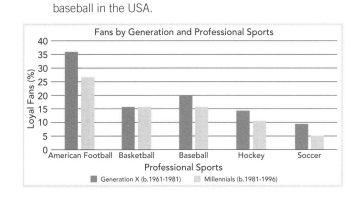

Fans by Generation and Professional Sports
Loyal Fans (%)
Professional Sports
■ Generation X (b.1961-1981) ■ Millennials (b.1981-1996)

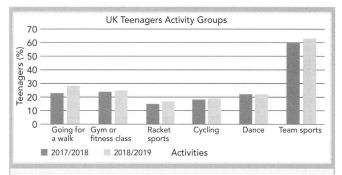

UK Teenagers Activity Groups
Teenagers (%)
Going for a walk | Gym or fitness class | Racket sports | Cycling | Dance | Team sports
■ 2017/2018 ■ 2018/2019 Activities

1 Staying active is important for teenagers so that they can be healthy and also have fun with their friends. So how do their free time activities help them stay healthy, and are they doing the same activities?

2 The bar chart looks at six different categories of activities that teenagers do after school. It is quantified in percentages, that is, the percentage of teenagers who take part in each type of activity. Some categories are comparable over the past few years, but others have changed a little.

3 It is important to note that the categories refer to activities that students do in their free time. It does not include activities at school, such as physical education lessons.

4 The most noticeable changes have occurred in the categories of team sports and going for a walk. Teenagers appear to be spending the same amount of time doing dance-related activities, but they are playing more team sports and going for more walks for pleasure.

5 It is important to remember that these are not the only ways teenagers spend their time being active. For example, the chart doesn't mention informal activity, like walking to school or playing with younger siblings at home. Do you think teenagers are more active now than they were in the past? The world is constantly changing, so it will be interesting to see what the future brings.

3 WRITING

a Look at the bar chart in 2a again. Then write an article about how millennials follow sport today. Use the notes to help you.

- more options – sports fans now follow more sports but watch fewer complete games
- different priorities – people have shorter attention spans
- TV – not as popular today; time may be inconvenient
- Internet – apps and social media provide instant access and news all the time
- lifestyle – single millennials without kids spend less time at home

1 READING

a Read the article about one of the greatest runners of all time. Tick (✓) the statements that are true.

1 ☐ Johnson's running style was considered strange.
2 ☐ Johnson had the potential to win more than he did.
3 ☐ Johnson loved the attention he got from his success.
4 ☐ Johnson had a different style from Usain Bolt.

b Read the article again and tick (✓) the correct answers.

1 The fact that Michael Johnson's friends laughed at his running style made him want to run even faster.
  a ☐ true   c ✓ doesn't say
  b ☐ false

2 It was considered surprising that Johnson was able to win both the 200 and 400 metres.
  a ☐ true   c ☐ doesn't say
  b ☐ false

3 Johnson was the first person to win the 400 metres at one Olympic Games and then win it again in the following Olympic Games.
  a ☐ true   c ☐ doesn't say
  b ☐ false

4 Johnson was injured during the 1988 Olympic Games.
  a ☐ true   c ☐ doesn't say
  b ☐ false

5 Johnson didn't race in the 200 metres final at the Barcelona Olympics.
  a ☐ true   c ☐ doesn't say
  b ☐ false

6 Johnson often refused to speak to journalists when he was very famous.
  a ☐ true   c ☐ doesn't say
  b ☐ false

7 Johnson now says that he might have been more successful if he'd been as relaxed as Usain Bolt.
  a ☐ true   c ☐ doesn't say
  b ☐ false

8 Usain Bolt tried to beat Johnson's 400 metres world record.
  a ☐ true   c ☐ doesn't say
  b ☐ false

c Write a paragraph about someone who has achieved a lot. Remember to include:

• some basic information about the person
• what they achieved and how they achieved it
• what other people think of them.

MICHAEL JOHNSON
THE MAN IN THE GOLDEN SHOES

Michael Johnson is one of the most successful professional athletes of all time. He won four Olympic gold medals and eight World Championship golds. People used to think that it was impossible for the same person to win the 200 metres as well as the 400 metres, but Johnson won both at the 1996 Atlanta Olympics, setting a new world record for both – 19.32 seconds and 43.49 seconds. He then went on to win the 400 metres again in Sydney in 2000 – the first time anyone had ever won the race in two Olympic Games in a row.

Anyone who saw Johnson perform in a race – even on TV – will remember him. He was an outstanding athlete, of course, but he also had a very unusual running style – short steps and a very straight back. When he was a child, his friends used to laugh at him because of how he ran. They said it was funny. Johnson later said he'd found it funny, too, but for another reason – the style was helping him win all his races.

Many people think that, with better luck, Johnson might have won even more medals – he was expected to be part of the team that went to the 1988 Olympics, but he had an injury and wasn't selected. Then in 1992, he got ill after eating in a restaurant two weeks before the start of the Barcelona Olympics. As a result, he didn't get as far as the 200 metres final, which he had been expected to win. In 1996, he avoided bad luck and the success story began.

Johnson's success made him rich and famous, and he was one of the first athletics 'superstars' – well known to the general public around the world, not just to athletics fans. But he didn't always seem to enjoy the fame – he sometimes sounded bad-tempered in interviews and, with the golden shoes that he started to wear when racing, some called him arrogant. After retiring, he explained that he'd found the press attention annoying.

Johnson, of course, had a natural talent for running, but many people say that it was his ability to focus and his dedication to training that made him so exceptional. The big running star of modern times – Usain Bolt – was famously relaxed, almost the opposite of Johnson. Whether Johnson could have run faster if he'd taken Bolt's more relaxed approach is up for debate – Johnson has said he certainly doesn't think so.

Johnson lost his 200 metres world record to Bolt and encouraged him to try the 400 metres as well, even though this could have lost Johnson his world record. One thing is for sure – it would be fascinating to know who would win a race between Bolt and Johnson at their best.

⊙ Review and extension

1 GRAMMAR

Tick (✓) the correct sentences. Correct the wrong sentences.

1 ☐ The police are trying to check who stole the money.
   The police are trying to find out who stole the money.
2 ☐ He's too young. He's still growing up.
3 ☐ It's warm. Put your jumper off.
4 ☐ We're finding a new secretary at the moment.
5 ☐ What ideas have you come up with?
6 ☐ Monica wasn't told about it yet.
7 ☐ Don't worry. I already sent the letter.
8 ☐ I'm waiting for you for ages!
9 ☐ I'm sure you've heard of the Loch Ness Monster.
10 ☐ I don't know. I didn't decide yet.

2 LISTENING

a ▶ 03.07 Listen to a conversation between two friends about their school days. Match names 1–5 with a–e to make sentences.

1 ☐ Julia   a argued with Mark.
2 ☐ Martina   b believed in Mark.
3 ☐ Mr Edwards   c was good at maths.
4 ☐ Sarah   d was good at sport.
5 ☐ Mrs Taylor   e was good at teaching grammar.

b Listen again. Look at the opinions. Who has these opinions – Tina, Mark or both? Tick (✓) the correct box.

	Tina	Mark	Both Mark and Tina
1 Martina is likely to have a successful career now.			✓
2 Julia was not friendly.			
3 Mr Edwards was a very good teacher.			
4 Sarah didn't have a good relationship with anybody at the school.			
5 Learning French at school wasn't very enjoyable.			
6 The school trips were not always educational.			

c Write a conversation between two people discussing their school days. Person A tells Person B about a subject they were good at. Person B tells Person A about a subject they were bad at. Use these questions to help you:

- Why was Person A good at their school subject?
- Was Person A naturally good at the school subject, or did they have to study hard?
- Why was Person B bad at their school subject?
- Is Person B good at this school subject now?

2 VOCABULARY

Tick (✓) the correct sentences. Correct the wrong sentences.

1 ☐ What are the secrets of success people?
   What are the secrets of successful people?
2 ☐ It's not able to get there by public transport.
3 ☐ No one doubts her capacity to get to the very top.
4 ☐ It was another fantastic performance by the Kenyan.
5 ☐ There is a training course for all new staff tomorrow.
6 ☐ Professional sport is very competitive.
7 ☐ What did the spectators think of the film?
8 ☐ The football players are just coming out on to the court.

3 WORDPOWER *up*

Read the sentences. Write *up* in the correct places.

1 We came early, but Greg turned late.
  We came early, but Greg turned up late.
2 If you don't know it, look it online.
3 She thought about it and decided not to bring the matter.
4 I used it all yesterday, so I went and bought some more.
5 We looked at the bill and added it again.
6 I went running with Percem, but I couldn't keep with her.
7 I started to learn Spanish and picked it pretty quickly.
8 He works so hard and I've always looked to him.

⟳ REVIEW YOUR PROGRESS

Look again at Review Your Progress on p. 42 of the Student's Book. How well can you do these things now?
3 = very well   2 = well   1 = not so well

I CAN ...	
discuss ability and achievement	☐
discuss sports activities and issues	☐
make careful suggestions	☐
write a description of data.	☐

4A | I'M MORE CAUTIOUS THAN I USED TO BE

1 GRAMMAR *used to* and *would*

a Underline the correct words to complete the sentences.

1 Yesterday my boss *used to come* / <u>came</u> to work late.
2 People *used to* / *would* believe the Sun went round the Earth.
3 One hundred years ago, it *couldn't* / *wouldn't* snow at all in winter.
4 We *lived* / *would live* in a small town before we moved to Istanbul.
5 I *would* / *used to* have a car, but I sold it.
6 That really *wasn't* / *didn't use to be* the best decision.
7 Julia *is used to working* / *used to work* in a shop before she started her own business.
8 Sam *would* / *got used to* stay up late every night studying when he was a university student.
9 I *wasn't used to* / *got used to* getting up so early, so the first morning was a shock.
10 It took me a long time to *be* / *get* used to wearing a uniform at work.

b ▶ 04.01 <u>Underline</u> the correct words to complete the text. Then listen and check.

Richard Morgan lives on a boat on a canal in London, but his life ¹*would* / *used to* / *was used to* be very different. Richard ²*left* / *used to leave* / *would leave* university in 2015 and got a great job at a law firm. It was interesting and well paid, but a very hard job. Richard ³*was used to* / *got used to* / *used to* work 12 to 14 hours a day and sometimes he ⁴*would sleep* / *was used to sleeping* / *got used to sleeping* at the office because it was so late. Richard ⁵*used to realise* / *would realise* / *realised* that this kind of life was killing him. 'I ⁶*was used to* / *used to* / *would* spending all my time at work. It was normal for me, that was the frightening thing,' Richard says.

On Sundays, Richard ⁷*used to going* / *got used to go* / *would go* for a walk down the canal and he always enjoyed this. So one day, when he had had enough, he ⁸*decided* / *used to decide* / *was used to deciding* to change his life completely. He gave up his job, bought a boat and said goodbye to his stressful life as a lawyer. 'It was a big contrast. I still haven't ⁹*used to* / *got used to* / *been used to* the ducks waking me up, but it's a great life,' he says. 'My family and friends were shocked at first, but now they ¹⁰*get used to visiting* / *are used to visiting* / *used to visiting* me on my boat and they know I'm happy.'

2 VOCABULARY Cause and result

a Correct the mistake in each sentence.

1 Smoking can lead in a lot of health problems.
   <u>Smoking can lead to a lot of health problems.</u>
2 No one knows what the affect was.
   _____
3 That's the main cause for the problem.
   _____
4 It could effect millions of people.
   _____
5 As a result from this, there is less money to spend.
   _____
6 The new law resulted of protests and demonstrations.
   _____
7 Generally, it's had a positive effect in people.
   _____

b Complete the text with the words in the box.

affect   as a result   ~~cause~~   effect
is caused by   lead   result

What makes people unhappy? Some people think that the biggest ¹___cause___ is stress, whether from work or the pressures of life. Certainly, lifestyle has a heavy influence on happiness. For example, a poor diet can ²_____ your health and ³_____ in illness and disease. Some people also think that unhappiness ⁴_____ loneliness. Friends do have a positive ⁵_____ on people's lives because friends provide support, entertainment and company. It's more complicated with family because relationships are often difficult and ⁶_____ can ⁷_____ to conflict and stress. This is clearly a difficult question to answer.

4B WE WEREN'T ALLOWED TO TALK IN CLASS

1 GRAMMAR Obligation and permission

a Complete the conversation with the responses in the box.

> I had to catch the 5:30 train.
> I'm tired during the day.
> No, I can work from home on Fridays.
> No, I don't have to unless we have a deadline.
> ~~No, I had to get up at 5:00 this morning.~~
> Yes, I can find a seat on the train.
> Yes, the boss lets us have one day at home.
> You should speak to my boss!

JANE Are you feeling all right?
ALEX ¹ No, I had to get up at 5:00 this morning.
JANE Why was that?
ALEX ²_____
JANE Do you do this every morning?
ALEX ³_____
JANE Is that the same for everyone?
ALEX ⁴_____
JANE Are there any advantages of getting to work early?
ALEX ⁵_____
JANE And the disadvantages?
ALEX ⁶_____
JANE Do you need to work late as well?
ALEX ⁷_____
JANE You need to ask for a pay rise.
ALEX ⁸_____

b Underline the correct words to complete the sentences.

1 It's for girls only, so he *can* / *can't* / *has to* take part in the competition.
2 You really *can* / *ought to* / *don't have to* read this book about Jackie Chan. It's brilliant.
3 Lola *mustn't* / *doesn't have to* / *shouldn't* train hard because she is very talented.
4 You *shouldn't* / *don't have to* / *are not allowed to* get nervous before the race.
5 The competition *was supposed* / *had* / *ought* to start at 7:00, but everyone was late.
6 Don't worry, you *mustn't* / *shouldn't* / *don't need to* train today.
7 My trainer made me *run* / *to run* / *running* ten kilometres.
8 During training, we're not allowed *eat* / *to eat* / *eating* certain food.
9 Don't let them *beat* / *to beat* / *beating* you in the race!
10 They were *let* / *allowed to* / *forced to* train in the cold and rain, even though they didn't want to.

2 VOCABULARY Talking about difficulty

a Underline the correct adjectives for the pictures.

1 a(n) *arduous* / *strict* journey
2 *tricky* / *rigorous* testing
3 *testing* / *strict* discipline

4 a(n) *tricky* / *exhausting* training schedule
5 *tough* / *punishing* standards
6 a *tricky* / *gruelling* situation

b Underline the correct words to complete the conversation.

KATE So what's it like to be a firefighter, William?
WILLIAM It's really ¹*straightforward* / *strict* / *tough*, much harder than I thought. The training is very ²*rigorous* / *awkward* / *delicate* and the instructors really ³*struggle* / *stretch* / *demand* us.
KATE But you've finished all the training?
WILLIAM Not yet. It's not so ⁴*strict* / *demanding* / *straightforward* to become a firefighter. First, there's this ⁵*arduous* / *straightforward* / *delicate* training schedule and then a ⁶*gruelling* / *tricky* / *backbreaking* written test to do at the end.
KATE Well, you do like a ⁷*struggle* / *punishment* / *challenge*! It sounds like a very ⁸*rigorous* / *demanding* / *tricky* job.

c ▶04.02 Listen and check.

3 PRONUNCIATION
Sound and spelling: *u*

a ▶04.03 Listen to the words in the box. How is the underlined letter *u* pronounced in each word? Complete the table with the words.

> ~~umbrella~~ pullover useless sugar supper
> attitude result influential enthusiasm

Sound 1 /ʌ/ (e.g., *cup*)	Sound 2 /ʊ/ (e.g., *cook*)	Sound 3 /uː/ or /juː/ (e.g., *food* or *cube*)
umbrella		

4C EVERYDAY ENGLISH
Thank you, you've saved my life

1 CONVERSATION SKILLS
Expressing careful disagreement

a Complete the table with the phrases in the box.

> I don't agree with you.
> Really, do you think so?
> That's just not true.
> Oh, I don't know.
> Maybe you're right, but …
> You can't really believe that.
> I know what you mean, but on the other hand …
> No way!
> I'm not sure about that.
> I'm afraid you're wrong there.

Careful disagreement	Direct disagreement
	I don't agree with you.

b Complete the conversation with the sentences in the box.

> I know what you mean, but on the other hand, technology is so central.
> Really, do you think so?
> I'm not sure about that. They work very hard.
> Oh, I don't know. Some things are improving.
> Maybe you're right, but teachers are not the real problem.

MARK Education is getting worse and worse in this country.

LILY ¹Oh, I don't know. Some things are improving.

MARK Like what? Teachers don't know what they're doing.

LILY ² _____

MARK Yes, but they need more training.

LILY ³ _____

MARK True – kids just don't want to study.

LILY ⁴ _____

MARK I do. They spend far too much time playing on their phones.

LILY ⁵ _____

MARK Hang on, someone's texting me …

c ▶ 04.04 Listen and check.

2 PRONUNCIATION Contrastive stress

a ▶ 04.05 Listen to the exchanges. <u>Underline</u> the word in each response with the strongest stress.

1 **A** It was an absolutely terrible hotel! I never want to go there again.
   B Oh, I don't know. It wasn't that bad.
2 **A** I really didn't like that film. It was so boring!
   B Oh, I don't know. It wasn't that boring.
3 **A** I loved that restaurant. The menu was really original.
   B Oh, I don't know. It wasn't that original.
4 **A** Have you seen that new shop? It looks great!
   B Oh, I don't know. It doesn't look that great.
5 **A** I thought the meeting today was far too long.
   B Oh, I don't know. It wasn't that long.

4D | SKILLS FOR WRITING
I'm good at communicating with people

Do you want to learn new skills and live and work in a beautiful environment? Volunteer to work as a forest ranger in a variety of locations with Forest Conservation Alliance.

RESPONSIBILITIES
You will carry out work around the forest, protect the environment and provide help to visitors and the general public.

What we offer you
- free accommodation
- training and education
- the opportunity to learn new skills

QUALIFICATIONS
You care about the environment and are a good team worker. You have a basic knowledge of a subject related to the environment.
You have good oral and written communication skills in English.

Re: Volunteers

Dear Forest Conservation Alliance,

I saw the advert for volunteers to work as forest rangers, and I would like to apply.

I am a student of environmental science in Turin, and I have travelled to the UK many times, so my language skills are very strong. I am also a friendly and sociable person who enjoys working with people.

As a student, I am in an excellent position to explain the beauty of the forest to visitors and to protect the forest from damage. I strongly believe that forests are essential for the world to survive, and it is the work of rangers to make people aware of this.

In our studies we have field trips to forests to study their natural beauty. I also spend a lot of my free time outdoors exploring. I am sure this knowledge and enthusiasm would help me in this position.

I am confident that I can be an important part of your team. I am reliable and hardworking, so this challenge is ideal for me. When I finish university, I would like to work in this field, so this is a wonderful opportunity.

I look forward to hearing from you.

Best regards,
Carla Rossini

1 READING

a Read the job advert and Carla's email. Then complete the summary with the words in the box.

fluently	forests	outside	people
~~ranger~~	reliable	strong	student

Carla wants to apply for a job as a ¹___ranger___. She is a
²_____ and speaks English ³_____. Carla
loves spending time ⁴_____ in ⁵_____ and
other interesting places. She likes to work with
⁶_____ and describes herself as ⁷_____.
Carla sounds like a ⁸_____ candidate.

b Read the advert and the email again. Are the sentences true or false?

1 There are several places to work.
2 You don't need to find somewhere to live.
3 Carla has only been to the UK once.
4 She has finished her studies.
5 Carla thinks that the world will not survive without forests.
6 She has some practical experience.
7 Carla is worried about the responsibility.
8 In the future, she wants to be a ranger.

2 WRITING SKILLS
Giving a positive impression

a Add the correct missing word to each sentence.

1 I would _____like_____ to apply to be a volunteer at the Winter Olympics.
2 I have always been interested _____ sports.
3 I would be more than happy to _____ up my free time.
4 I am in an excellent _____ to help athletes and visitors.
5 I _____ believe that sport brings people together.
6 I look _____ to hearing from you.

3 WRITING

a Read the advert and the plan. Then write an application email.

Do you want to be part of an international team and support the world's greatest sporting event? Become a volunteer at the Winter Olympics with Olympics United!

Responsibilities
There are a range of opportunities depending on your experience and skills, such as preparing food for athletes, helping in the medical centre and interpreting.

What we offer you
- free accommodation
- tickets to events
- the opportunity to learn new skills

Qualifications
You are physically fit.

You have good oral and written communication skills in English.

 **Apply for this job**

 Save to favourites

Plan
Paragraph 1: reason for writing
Paragraph 2: your background (work / education), your communication skills
Paragraph 3: your experience, personality and other skills, how these make you a good candidate
Paragraph 4: why you want to be a volunteer, your interest in sport / the Olympics
Paragraph 5: closing sentence

BLOG

Train journeys and unwritten rules

[posted by Paul, yesterday at 7:14 pm]

Well, I've just arrived home furious! Why? Something quite silly, really, but very annoying. As most of you reading probably know, I commute to work every day by train. Today, I was standing with a few other people by the train doors as the train arrived at the station. Now, what's supposed to happen is that people get off the train first, and then the people who are on the platform get on. It works better that way. It's the logical way to do it. But today, as soon as the doors opened, everyone on the platform started to get on, and we had to kind of fight our way off. There was no advantage for the people on the platform to get on the train first – they still had to wait for everyone else to get off, and it just created confusion, although I suppose they were worried about finding a seat on the train. While it was all happening, I got angry and ended up having an argument with someone getting on.

Anyway, it got me thinking. There's no rule anywhere that says that the people on the platform are supposed to wait and let the people on the train get off first. That's just what people do. It's an unwritten rule. So, what other unwritten rules can you think of? Do you ever see people breaking them? And if so, what do you do?

COMMENTS

Sam: yesterday at 7:43 pm
Exactly the same problem on the bus recently. Everyone tries to get on without letting anyone off first! It doesn't make sense – what's the hurry?

Irene: yesterday at 11:11 pm
Another unwritten rule? Queuing! There are some places, like clothes shops, where there are actually barriers that make you queue, but generally we just do it without thinking. And if someone jumps the queue? Generally I say nothing – at most I tend to give them a dirty look, but that's a waste of time because they're already in front of me in the line and can't see my face!

Sara: today at 9:11 am
I suppose politely holding a door open for someone is another unwritten rule. It's funny because I think sometimes it would be easier for everyone not to – if the other person isn't directly behind you, you have to wait for them, and also they have to hurry so you're not waiting too long! But I always do it. If someone doesn't hold the door open for me, then I think they're rude.

Juan: today at 11:15 am
Tipping is an unwritten rule, but I find that the rule changes a lot depending on the country! I grew up in a country where you'd only leave money if you thought the waiter was really good or you had a great time. But when I visited the USA, I learnt that there everyone leaves 15% to 20%, even if the service isn't that good. I prefer the unwritten rule in my country!

1 READING

a Read the blog post and comments. Tick (✓) the things that are <u>not</u> mentioned by the writer or in the comments.

1. ☐ Behaviour on public transport
2. ☐ Queuing
3. ☐ Doing something to be polite
4. ☐ Regretting doing something rude
5. ☐ Paying extra for something

b Read the blog and comments again. Write the names of the people.

1. Which person mentions something they do that is pointless? _____
2. Which person compares a situation in two different countries? _____
3. Which person cannot understand a particular behaviour of other people? _____
4. Which person describes a polite form of behaviour that may have a negative result? _____
5. Which person suggests they may understand why rude behaviour took place? _____

c Read the blog and comments again. Are the sentences true or false?

1. The original writer, Paul, was involved in a violent situation.
2. Paul believes there needs to be a written rule to tell people to wait before getting on the train.
3. Irene doesn't normally argue with people who jump the queue.
4. Sara doesn't expect people to hold the door open for her.
5. Juan doesn't like tipping practices in the USA.

d Write a paragraph about an 'unwritten rule' in your country or a country you know well. You should say:

- what the rule is
- whether you think the rule is necessary
- what you or other people tend to do when the rule is broken.

2 LISTENING

a ▶ 04.06 Listen to some interviews with university graduates. How many are unhappy with their final grades at university? Tick (✓) the correct answer.

1 ☐ one student   3 ☐ three students
2 ☐ two students   4 ☐ all four students

b Listen again and tick (✓) the correct answers.

1   What do we learn about Carl's year?
    a ☐ He studied a lot during this period.
    b ☐ He had to buy a lot of books.
    c ☐ He was very busy at work.

2   Why did Carl find his experience at university difficult?
    a ☐ He had to pay a lot for his studies.
    b ☐ He has a young family to look after.
    c ☐ He had to work and study at the same time.

3   Why did Samantha mention that she had three exams in two days?
    a ☐ to show that this was really the only difficulty she had
    b ☐ because she is unhappy with the university administration
    c ☐ to explain how little control you have over your timetable as a student

4   Why didn't Luke get the final grade he wanted?
    a ☐ He had a bad cold during the last two exams.
    b ☐ His performance on his final two exams wasn't strong enough.
    c ☐ He was seriously ill on the day of one exam.

5   Which of the following opinions does Luke express?
    a ☐ He doesn't think that you should have to take an exam if you are really ill.
    b ☐ He is sure he would have got the marks he wanted if he hadn't been ill.
    c ☐ He thinks the university shouldn't consider illness only on the day of an exam.

6   Which of the following statements best matches something Jane says?
    a ☐ You need to get a lot of sleep to succeed at university.
    b ☐ It's harder to get a degree if you don't have friends or family who have studied at university.
    c ☐ It's better to go to university before you're 40.

7   What do we learn about Jane's work situation?
    a ☐ She hopes she will get a chance to progress more at work now that she's graduated.
    b ☐ She's found a new job since she graduated.
    c ☐ She thinks it's going to be hard to find a job even though she now has a university degree.

c Write about an event that has had a big influence on your life. Use these questions to help you:

- What was the event?
- Why was it important for you?
- What was your life like before the event?
- How did your life change after the event?

⊙ Review and extension

1 GRAMMAR

Tick (✓) the correct sentences. Correct the wrong sentences.

1 ☐ My granddad use to work in a factory near Manchester.
     My granddad used to work in a factory near Manchester.
2 ☐ I would prefer to see my own doctor.
3 ☐ She used to living by herself now.
4 ☐ This can be the last time we come here.
5 ☐ I hope we could do this again some time.
6 ☐ If you want to apply, you should fill out this form.

2 VOCABULARY

Tick (✓) the correct sentences. Correct the wrong sentences.

1 ☐ Sunday is better cause I'm free then.
     Sunday is better because I'm free then.
2 ☐ I'm worried that it might effect my health.
3 ☐ It can lead to all kinds of problems.
4 ☐ My first teacher was very strickt.
5 ☐ She left because she felt she needed a new challenge.
6 ☐ Prisons are basically for punish criminals.

3 WORDPOWER *as*

Underline the correct words to complete the sentences.

1   The rules of the game are as *follows* / *a whole* – first, there must be at least five players.
2   It looks as *a matter of fact* / *if* we were all wrong.
3   There's a lot to do there as *far as* / *for* entertainment is concerned.
4   The competition was good for the country as *a whole* / *follows* – everyone benefited.
5   She's still on holiday as far as *I'm concerned* / *I know*.
6   The tickets are too expensive and as far as *I'm concerned* / *I know*, they're a waste of money.
7   More people live in the UK than in Spain. As *a whole* / *a matter of fact*, the population is almost 67 million.
8   Alice is very nice, but as *for* / *if* her husband – well, he's rather strange.

🔄 REVIEW YOUR PROGRESS

Look again at Review Your Progress on p. 54 of the Student's Book. How well can you do these things now?

3 = very well   2 = well   1 = not so well

I CAN ...	
discuss events that changed my life	☐
discuss and describe rules	☐
describe photos	☐
write an email to apply for work.	☐

5A YOU COULD LIVE TO BE A HUNDRED

1 GRAMMAR Future probability

a Underline the correct words to complete the conversation.

KATY Have you read this article, Josh? It says there's a good [1]*chance* / *doubt* the next generation will live to be 150 years old!

JOSH Who knows, what it says [2]*may* / *will* be true. But what evidence is there?

KATY Advances in medicine [3]*might* / *will* certainly be a factor, and people [4]*won't* / *couldn't* die from all sorts of diseases common today. Also, technology [5]*will probably* / *probably will* make everyday life easier.

JOSH Fine, but I [6]*don't suppose* / *doubt* if many people will want to live that long. It's [7]*unlikely* / *sure* that it'll be much fun to be 150.

KATY The article says that we [8]*may* / *will* probably be able to work until that age. There's a good chance [9]*of* / *that* machines [10]*will* / *won't* do all the hard work, like washing and cleaning, so that we can do different tasks, like critical thinking.

JOSH Interesting. I'm [11]*probable* / *sure* there'll even be a special Olympics for people over 100!

KATY Yes, it's bound [12]*to happen* / *happen*, so start training!

b ▶ 05.01 Listen and check.

c Tick (✓) the correct words to complete the sentences.

1 Pollution _____ be even worse in the future if we don't start taking responsibility for it.
   a ✓ will probably b ☐ probably will c ☐ likely will

2 I'm sure that it _____ happen in our lifetime.
   a ☐ may not b ☐ might not c ☐ won't

3 Virtual reality _____ become more popular, but I doubt it.
   a ☐ might b ☐ will c ☐ can

4 The question is _____ we find a real solution to our energy problems?
   a ☐ may b ☐ might c ☐ will

5 Cinemas _____ go out of business in the future.
   a ☐ probably will c ☐ won't probably
   b ☐ will probably

6 It's unlikely _____ computers will replace teachers.
   a ☐ for b ☐ if c ☐ that

7 There's no _____ that they will stop printing books.
   a ☐ likely b ☐ probability c ☐ chance

8 I can't _____ that one day we will be able to go on holiday to the Moon.
   a ☐ imagine b ☐ suppose c ☐ guess

9 Airport security is sure _____ change with new technology.
   a ☐ to b ☐ that c ☐ of

10 Productivity at work is _____ to get better soon now that we can work from home.
   a ☐ possible b ☐ bound c ☐ probable

2 VOCABULARY Adjectives describing attitude

a Complete the words.

1 How r e a l i s t i c is it that we'll live to 150 years old? I mean will it actually happen?
2 Sam is always late handing in work. He's completely u_ r _ _ _ _ b _e.
3 It was an u _ _ y _ _ _ _ _ e _ _ c comment, and he immediately felt sorry he'd said it.
4 Victoria is really a_ v _ _ _ _ r _ _ s. She's just gone on a trekking holiday in the Ecuadorian rainforest.
5 Wendy is really t _ _ _ _ _ _ f _ _, so she will always check on you when you're ill or upset about something.
6 You can tell he's w_ _l o _ _ _ _ _s _ d by looking at how tidy his desk is.

b Complete the sentences with the words in the box. There are four extra words you do not need.

adventurous ambitious cautious ~~critical~~
disorganised irresponsible reliable thoughtful
uncompetitive unrealistic unsympathetic

1 He's very _critical_ of the way the work was done.
2 I've never known anyone so _____; you can never count on him.
3 It's dangerous out there; I guess it's better to be _____ and play it safe.
4 Even if the place is a bit _____, we still know where everything is.
5 I may be _____ compared to everyone else, but I still want to win.
6 That was a really _____ trip – you won't believe all the incredible things that happened.
7 The new waiter is obviously very _____. I've never seen anyone work as hard as him.

3 PRONUNCIATION Sound and spelling: *th*

a How are the underlined letters *th* pronounced in each word in the box? Complete the table with the words.

a<u>th</u>letic brea<u>th</u> brea<u>th</u>ing mo<u>th</u>er Ear<u>th</u> ei<u>th</u>er
lea<u>th</u>er leng<u>th</u> mon<u>th</u> <u>th</u>e ~~<u>th</u>ink~~ <u>th</u>ough

Sound 1 /θ/ (e.g., *th*ank)	Sound 2 /ð/ (e.g., *th*en)
think	

b ▶ 05.02 Listen and check.

28

5B | I'LL BE SETTLING INTO MY ACCOMMODATION

1 GRAMMAR Future perfect and future continuous

a Underline the correct words to complete the sentences.

1 Passengers, we will soon *be arriving* / *have arrived* at the station.
2 You can still help because they won't *have finished* / *be finishing* yet.
3 Will polar bears still *be living* / *have lived* 50 years from now?
4 We'll *be feeding* / *have fed* the penguins at 2:30, so make sure you see that.
5 The team will *have completed* / *be completing* their project by 2031.
6 What will we *be achieving* / *have achieved* after we've spent all this money on research?
7 I don't think we'll *have driven* / *be driving* cars in 20 years' time.
8 Fleur will *be learning* / *have learned* a lot by the time she leaves Antarctica.
9 This time tomorrow, I'll *be getting* / *have got* ready to go.
10 Fleur will be glad to get back because she won't *be seeing* / *have seen* her friends for ages.

b Complete the text with the future continuous or future perfect forms of the verbs in the box.

> change   complain   not cook   create   destroy
> not eat   not fall   go   ~~not live~~   replace   study
> transport   turn   walk

Let's travel to the year 2059! We ^{1}**won't be living** on Earth because pollution and wars ^{2}_____ the old planet. Instead, planet Zeus will be our home. Giant spaceships ^{3}_____ everyone and everything from Earth before it exploded in 2055. Zeus won't be a bad place to live, and some things will go on as normal. Adults ^{4}_____ to work every morning. Children ^{5}_____ at school and old people ^{6}_____ about almost everything. Many things will be different, though. Because of the different atmosphere, our hair ^{7}_____ green – at least it ^{8}_____ out – and we ^{9}_____ about in space suits. Special tablets ^{10}_____ food and drink, so we ^{11}_____ at all, and we ^{12}_____ out at restaurants. Yes, life ^{13}_____ quite a lot.
Welcome to 2059 and the future we ^{14}_____.

c ▶ 05.03 Listen and check.

2 VOCABULARY The natural world

a Match 1–7 with a–g to make sentences.

1 [e] Big companies don't seem to worry enough about the ecological
2 [ ] There was a period of rough
3 [ ] There are people who think that climate
4 [ ] We make an effort to be environmentally
5 [ ] Just look at the river to see the effect of global
6 [ ] We don't realise that we live in a fragile
7 [ ] I read that solar

a change is some kind of myth.
b energy is one of the fastest growing forms of energy.
c environment and everything is interconnected.
d friendly, but it's not always easy.
e impact of what they do.
f warming on water levels.
g weather and we couldn't go out much.

b Complete the words.

1 Global w**arming**_____ is changing animals' natural habitats.

2 Cities are trying to be more environmentally f_____.

3 Obviously, s_____ energy is a cleaner alternative than oil and gas.

4 Tourism can damage the desert's fragile e_____.

5 We can reduce our carbon f_____ by taking fewer flights.

6 It would be crazy to go out to sea in this r_____ weather.

7 Recent winters have been colder as a result of c_____ change.

8 Just stop and think about the ecological i_____ of how we live.

5C EVERYDAY ENGLISH
We're not making enough money

1 USEFUL LANGUAGE Discussing advantages and disadvantages

a <u>Underline</u> the correct words to complete the conversation.

MAGDA You know, I'm seriously thinking [1]*at / of / on* taking this job in Paris.

ROMAN No wonder! One good [2]*thing / advantage / problem* about it is the higher salary. It's basically a promotion.

MAGDA True, but the trouble [3]*by / for / with* that is more pressure and stress. A big disadvantage [4]*by / of / for* the position I've been offered is that I'll have too much to do.

ROMAN Come on, one of the best things [5]*about / with / of* you is how you respond to a challenge.

MAGDA I suppose so ... Another problem [6]*at / from / with* this job offer is that I'll need to improve my French – and fast!

ROMAN No need to worry [7]*for / at / about* that either. The advantage [8]*for / of / at* living and working in a foreign country is that you learn the language quickly.

MAGDA You have an answer to everything!

ROMAN The only drawback [9]*of / by / in* the job I can see is the size of the company. Do you really want to work in a company that big?

MAGDA If they pay me enough money, yes!

b ▶ 05.04 Listen and check.

2 CONVERSATION SKILLS Responding to an idea

a Complete the conversation with the responses in the box.

> That's a great idea! You haven't made one for ages.
> That's a possibility, although we might have to invite them in for a coffee or something.
> Hmm, I don't know about that. I'm not so keen on spicy food.
> That's not a bad idea. They'd need to drive there, though.
> Yes, that makes sense. I need the exercise!
> ~~It's an idea, I suppose. Where shall we go?~~
> That might be worth a try, and it's not far.

A How about eating out tonight for a change?
B [1]<u>It's an idea, I suppose. Where shall we go?</u>
A There's a new Thai place which has just opened.
B [2]_____
A Well, there's the Italian place just up the hill.
B [3]_____
A Let's walk there. It's a lovely day.
B [4]_____
A We could invite Amelia and Rob, too.
B [5]_____
A Then they could give us a lift if we feel too lazy to walk back.
B [6]_____
A So I've got an excuse to make one of your favourite lemon cakes.
B [7]_____

b ▶ 05.05 Listen and check.

3 PRONUNCIATION Intonation groups

a ▶ 05.06 Listen and <u>underline</u> the words that are stressed in the sentences.

1 The <u>trouble</u> <u>is</u> it could take a long time to get the money.
2 The good thing about it is we're not far away from the centre.
3 The problem is people are starting to talk about her.
4 The advantage is the price isn't very high.
5 The drawback is no one really knows what's going to happen.
6 The advantage is we can see a lot more of each other.
7 The trouble is I'm not sure I've got time to help him.
8 A definite disadvantage is it means selling the car.

5D SKILLS FOR WRITING
We need to change the way we live

People have always worried about population growth. It is a fact that the number of people on the planet is increasing very quickly, in some countries more than others. This puts a lot of pressure on the Earth's resources. But is population growth really leading to some kind of crisis?

Many people believe that we just cannot produce enough food to feed everyone. The increase in food prices is proof of this. Furthermore, clean drinking water is getting harder to find, a situation made worse by climate change.

However, not everyone agrees with these arguments. We could produce food much more efficiently with technology, and in the same way we could treat seawater to produce an almost endless supply of drinking water. Some people point out that our problem is distribution of resources, and this is something we can solve.

Overall, population growth is a concern, but there should be enough food and water for everyone if we become more efficient. My own view is that we can't do much about our increasing population, but we can make sure the way we produce and distribute resources is as effective and fair as possible.

Page 1 of 1   192 words   110%

1 READING

a Read the essay and complete the summary with the words in the box.

> against   conclusion   crisis   ~~essay~~
> for   growth   manage

This ¹___essay___ discusses whether population
²_____ is a problem. It considers arguments first
³_____ and then ⁴_____ the idea and comes
to the ⁵_____ that there won't be any major
⁶_____ if we ⁷_____ resources properly.

b Read the essay again. Are the sentences true or false?

1 Population growth is a new concern.
2 Food prices are rising.
3 The shortage of water is causing climate change.
4 There are ways of turning seawater into drinking water.
5 The real issue is how we share food and water.
6 The population will eventually stop growing.

2 WRITING SKILLS Arguing for and against an idea

a Are the arguments for or against giving aid to developing countries? Tick (✓) the correct box.

	For	Against
1 Some of the aid is lost and stolen.		✓
2 Wealth needs to be shared around the world.		
3 We have a moral responsibility to help people in need.		
4 Giving aid makes developing countries dependent.		
5 We have problems to worry about in our own country.		
6 Developing countries could become important markets or partners.		
7 It will mean fewer problems with illegal immigration.		
8 There are always rich and poor countries – that's just how things are.		

3 WRITING

a Write an essay for and against the topic 'Richer countries should give aid to developing countries.' Use the following structure:

- Introduction – state the problem
- Arguments for giving aid
- Arguments against giving aid
- Conclusion – summarise the main points and give your opinion

1 READING

a Read the article about optimistic people. Tick (✓) the correct summary of the author's ideas.

1 ☐ It's usually impossible to be an optimist if you are not naturally positive.

2 ☐ Anyone can be optimistic if they choose to do the right things.

3 ☐ Highly optimistic people are more fun to be with.

b Read the article again. Match topics a–e with paragraphs 1–5.

a ☐ Choosing the right things to think about

b ☐ Having ambitions can help

c ☐ Keeping a record

d ☐ Rethinking your attitude to work

e ☐ Where you are, who you're with

c Read the article again. Are the sentences true or false?

1 Optimists are both healthier and more successful at work.

2 Optimists focus on the happiness that the money they earn can bring.

3 It's easier to think about bad things that have happened to you than good things.

4 The writer suggests that if you believe in something enough, you'll definitely achieve what you want.

5 The writer says that writing a diary can help you understand your negative thoughts better.

6 The article says that optimistic people are lucky because they are naturally very positive.

d Write a paragraph about staying positive. Remember to include:

• what makes you feel positive
• what makes you feel less positive
• what you do if you want to improve your mood.

The five secrets of highly optimistic people

Everyone wants to be an optimist, but it's not always easy – most of us have to try hard to stay positive when life is getting us down. It's worth the effort, though, since optimists enjoy better health and even do better in their careers. Here are five things that optimists do that will help you look on the bright side, even when you're stuck in a traffic jam or forced to work on a Sunday.

The secret to optimism is that it doesn't just happen – highly optimistic people work hard to stay positive. If you want to do well in your career, improve your relationships and enjoy your life, it's time to give optimism a try.

1 Optimists are passionate about their work. Do you need to force yourself to go to work each morning? Optimists don't because they jump out of bed excited to face the day. This is because optimists have chosen jobs and careers that they genuinely feel passionate about. If you can't remember the last time you enjoyed a day at work, it may be time to start looking for a new job. For optimists, work is more than just an opportunity to earn money. It's also an opportunity to learn, grow and do what they love.

2 Optimists focus on good things, even though it's not the easiest thing to do. According to Florida State University professor Roy F. Baumeister's article, 'Bad Is Stronger Than Good,' it's much easier to focus on the rainy days than the sunny ones. In the paper, Baumeister says people are generally more upset about losing $50 than they are happy to gain $50. When you start to feel bad-tempered or depressed, think about something good from your day to balance out the negative emotions. Optimists make a choice to focus on the good in their life instead of thinking about the bad.

3 Optimists are more likely to be adventurous and ambitious. Believe in your dreams – and if you have big dreams, you might achieve better results. In 1997, researcher Gary McPherson studied child musicians, their goals and what happened to them later in life. He found that the child musicians who imagined themselves playing their instrument forever were more likely to become professional musicians in the future. So, while belief on its own isn't enough for success, a little dreaming certainly won't hurt.

4 Optimists keep a diary. As we've mentioned, it's very easy to focus on the negative events in our lives and ignore the positives. Keeping a diary can help you release negative energy and focus on positive emotions. During a few quiet moments in your morning or before bed, write a list of the positive moments from your day or things you're trying to achieve in the future.

5 Optimists surround themselves with good feelings. If you surround yourself with supportive people and things you enjoy, you'll improve your mood and your day. The next time you lose concentration and start looking at videos of cats and dogs on the Internet, don't feel so bad about the time you 'wasted'. Research has shown that spending a few moments doing something you enjoy will actually make you more productive.

2 LISTENING

a ▶ 05.07 Listen to a conversation between two friends, Andrew and Fran. Tick (✓) the things they talk about.

1 ☐ a new supermarket   4 ☐ food choices
2 ☐ packaging   5 ☐ technology
3 ☐ air travel   6 ☐ animal conservation

b Listen again and tick (✓) the correct answers.

1 What is unusual about the supermarket Fran mentions?
   a ☐ It has very low prices compared to other supermarkets.
   b ☐ It sells different kinds of things from most other supermarkets.
   c ✓ The way it sells things is different from other supermarkets.

2 Why wouldn't Andrew want to use a supermarket like this?
   a ☐ He thinks it would be too time-consuming to shop there.
   b ☐ He doesn't want to have to use his car to get there.
   c ☐ He thinks it's safer if products in the supermarket use packaging.

3 What problem does Fran <u>not</u> mention related to the use of packaging?
   a ☐ the pollution it causes when it is manufactured
   b ☐ the risk it causes to animals if they eat it
   c ☐ the fact that it is often not dealt with properly after it has been used

4 What does Fran say about the idea of never using a car?
   a ☐ It's probably impossible.
   b ☐ It's difficult, but not impossible.
   c ☐ Most people wouldn't agree to do it.

5 Which of the following statements is true about Andrew?
   a ☐ He didn't know about the positive environmental impact of vegetarianism.
   b ☐ He doesn't agree with people not eating meat.
   c ☐ He is going to try to reduce the amount of meat he eats.

6 Which of the following statements best summarises Fran's views on the environment?
   a ☐ We need to discuss what we can do to help the environment more often.
   b ☐ People in general aren't doing enough to help the environment.
   c ☐ People will probably start changing their behaviour when they realise how serious the situation is.

7 How hopeful is Fran about the chances of new technology solving environmental problems?
   a ☐ very hopeful
   b ☐ generally hopeful
   c ☐ not very hopeful

c Write an email to a newspaper about a global problem that you are worried about. For example, you could talk about how pollution is a major problem all over the world. Remember to include:
- a short description of the problem
- why the problem worries you
- a possible solution to the problem
- why the problem might be difficult to solve.

👁 Review and extension

1 GRAMMAR

Tick (✓) the correct sentences. Correct the wrong sentences.

1 ☐ Please write as soon as possible to me.
   Please write to me as soon as possible.
2 ☐ She probably has been waiting for this news all week.
3 ☐ Your trip to Antarctica won't certainly disappoint you.
4 ☐ It's not likely that she will persuade her parents.
5 ☐ What will we doing this time tomorrow?
6 ☐ We hope that the problem will have been solved.

2 VOCABULARY

Tick (✓) the correct sentences. Correct the wrong sentences.

1 ☐ We need someone responsable for this job.
   We need someone responsible for this job.
2 ☐ I always thought Tom was relyable until this latest incident.
3 ☐ I prefer to talk to Ann because she is more sympathetic.
4 ☐ If your desk is always neat, you're probably organised well.
5 ☐ Pollution has led to the climate change in many areas.
6 ☐ Most things we do leave some kind of carbon footprint.

3 WORDPOWER *side*

Complete the sentences with the expressions in the box.

both sides   from side to side   nice side
~~side by side~~   to one side

1 Developed countries need to work <u>side by side</u> to help the developing parts of the world.
2 Emma seems a little cold sometimes, but she definitely has her _____.
3 In this essay, you need to present _____ of the argument.
4 I was so scared – the boat was rocking _____ in the high winds.
5 The teacher took the child _____ and told her not to do it again.

🔄 REVIEW YOUR PROGRESS

Look again at Review Your Progress on p. 66 of the Student's Book. How well can you do these things now?
3 = very well   2 = well   1 = not so well

I CAN ...	
discuss possible future events	☐
prepare for a job interview	☐
discuss advantages and disadvantages	☐
write an argument for and against an idea.	☐

6A | I'M NOT GOING TO TRY TO SEE EVERYTHING

1 GRAMMAR Infinitives and -ing forms

a Underline the correct words to complete the conversation.

ELENA Hi, Max, glad [1]*to see* / *seeing* you. How's your summer?

MAX Boring! I'm looking forward to [2]*go* / *going* back to college. [3]*To sit* / *Sitting* in front of the computer all day is not my idea of a holiday.

ELENA Why don't you go somewhere [4]*to have* / *having* a break? I think it's really important [5]*to get* / *getting* away from everything once in a while.

MAX [6]*To travel* / *Travelling* is a waste of time. I remember [7]*to visit* / *visiting* Paris last spring. I tried [8]*to see* / *seeing* the *Mona Lisa* in the Louvre, but there were so many people I couldn't even get in the room, which was just as well as I'd forgotten [9]*to take* / *taking* my camera. Anyway, I'm not interested in [10]*walking* / *to walk* around in crowds of tourists.

ELENA Sorry [11]*hearing* / *to hear* that – but look, stop [12]*to be* / *being* so negative. You obviously like art – that's why you were in the Louvre – so why not do something connected with that? I can see you [13]*doing* / *to do* something creative.

MAX I've tried [14]*painting* / *to paint* and I wasn't too bad at it.

ELENA There you are, you may go on [15]*being* / *to be* in the Louvre yourself!

b ▶06.01 Listen and check.

c Complete the text with infinitive or gerund forms of the verbs in the box.

> admire continue cut have listen melt
> pour protect stop think ~~turn~~ visit

Welcome to Niagara Falls! This is your personal audio guidebook. Remember [1] _to turn_ the volume up quite high because it's pretty noisy here. You can hear the water [2]_____ down the Falls, millions of litres every minute. If you want [3]_____ the view, press the red button [4]_____ the guide, and then the blue button [5]_____ and go on [6]_____. It's amazing [7]_____ that the Falls have been here for 10,000 years. Basically, ice [8]_____ into the Niagara River made it powerful enough [9]_____ a huge piece out of the rock. More about this later. Back to today: millions of tourists come [10]_____ the Falls each year. [11]_____ so many visitors is great, but all the activity causes a lot of damage, so we are trying [12]_____ the Falls as much as possible. So …

d ▶06.02 Listen and check.

2 VOCABULARY Travel and tourism

a Read the definitions. Reorder the letters to make travel and tourism adjectives.

1	not easily forgotten	e m b o e a m r l	_memorable_
2	unusual and foreign	t o e x i c	_____
3	something you admire	i p e s v i m e r s	_____
4	extremely attractive	u n s g n t n i	_____
5	the only one of its kind	e u q i n u	_____
6	very high quality	e s b r u p	_____
7	really surprising	n a i s o s t i n h g	_____
8	very noticeable	a r m b a k e e r l	_____

b Complete the text with the words in the box. There are two extra words you do not need.

> features hiking lobby outskirts ~~setting~~
> structures terminal terrace venue

The Grovepark Hotel is located in a perfect [1] _setting_ on the [2]_____ of Casterbridge just half an hour away from the city centre and minutes from the [3]_____ trails going up into the Wessex Hills. It's an ideal conference [4]_____ with a number of [5]_____ delegates will appreciate. Whether you're outside relaxing on the [6]_____ admiring the views over your coffee, or inside in the [7]_____ bar, you'll feel completely at home.

c ▶06.03 Listen and check.

3 PRONUNCIATION Consonant clusters

a Look at the underlined syllables and decide if they contain 2, 3 or 4 consonant sounds. Tick (✓) the correct box.

		2	3	4
a	We had some su<u>perb</u> meals in an excellent local restaurant.	✓		
b	These ideas are a big con<u>trast</u> to what we heard yesterday.			
c	The Pyramids in Egypt are the most impressive <u>structures</u> I've ever seen.			
d	Their di<u>scuss</u>ion lasted two hours.			
e	We can't de<u>stroy</u> the original document.			
f	The <u>train</u> terminal is a short walk from the airport.			

b ▶06.04 Listen and check.

6B | ABOUT HALF THE WORLD'S LANGUAGES WILL DISAPPEAR

1 GRAMMAR The passive

a Underline the correct words to complete the text.

Speak any language in 30 days! That's right, with our new online course, any language can ¹*be learnt / have been learnt* effortlessly and perfectly. This is made possible ²*with / by* an amazing piece of software which today ³*has been used / is being used* by thousands of people studying 25 different languages in the comfort of their own homes.

It's so simple. All the work ⁴*is done / is being done* online, and the course is complete. No expensive extras have ⁵*to be bought / been bought*. But don't listen to us, listen to our customers:

'I ⁶*am promoted / was promoted* back in January, but I needed to improve my English. This course ⁷*has been recommended / had been recommended* to me by a colleague, so I bought it and the results were amazing! Now I ⁸*am considered / am being considered* for an overseas post, and I'm hoping my salary ⁹*will be increased / was increased*.' (Jackie Lee, 32)

'I ¹⁰*have been given / am given* a completely new direction in life by this course. Now I can communicate with people all over the world. I'm so glad I ¹¹*was persuaded / am persuaded* to sign up.' (Mabel Smith, 89)

What are you waiting for? Send us an email and you ¹²*are contacted / will be contacted* by our customer care team in 24 hours.

Goodbye! ¡Adios! Poka! Ciao!

b ▶️06.05 Listen and check.

c Complete the sentences with the correct passive form of the verbs in brackets.

1 English __is spoken__ (speak) all round the world nowadays.
2 The ancient manuscript _____ (write) thousands of years ago in an unknown dialect.
3 Many foreign words _____ (add) to English over the centuries.
4 And that was the last word to _____ (speak) in the language of Bo.
5 All the smaller languages _____ (lose) one day, which is very sad.
6 There are free online courses, but _____ people _____ (encourage) to take them?
7 A new online dictionary of medical terms _____ (made) for doctors at the moment.
8 The language _____ (not / hear) on the island for years before its revival began.
9 The pronunciation of any language _____ (make) out of a fixed number of possible sounds.
10 There is no doubt that grammar should _____ (teach) to children in schools today.

2 VOCABULARY Describing changes

a Underline the correct words to complete the sentences.

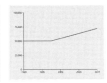

1 Membership numbers began to *decline / disappear* later in the period.

2 The dodo *deteriorated / died out* due to human interference.

3 As you can see, eventually viewing figures *decreased / increased*.

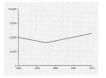

4 Happily, sales are starting to *decline / revive* after a disappointing start.

5 My relationship with my boss began to *deteriorate / preserve*.

6 The ship *died out / disappeared* at sea and was never seen again.

b Complete the conversation with the noun form of the words in brackets.

A Professor, why is it important to keep languages alive?
B Because the ¹ __survival__ (survive) of languages means the ² _____ (preserve) of cultures, too.
A Are there many languages being lost?
B You can see the ³ _____ (disappear) of smaller languages all the time.
A Can you give any examples?
B Belorussian, the language in Belarus, hasn't died out, but it is in decline and future ⁴ _____ (generate) might not speak it at all.
A What about the opposite?
B There has been a ⁵ _____ (revive) in the Celtic language of Cornish.
A But what causes language ⁶ _____ (lose)?
B Basically, ⁷ _____ (compete) with bigger languages. The increase in English as a major international language is a massive factor. The effect goes beyond just language.
A What do you mean?
B Well, globalisation can also mean a ⁸ _____ (deteriorate) in local customs.
A That sounds depressingly true.

c ▶️06.06 Listen and check.

1 USEFUL LANGUAGE
Introducing requests; Showing you are grateful

a Complete the exchanges with the sentences in the box.

Do you mind if I ask you to get my coat?
Great! I don't know how to thank you.
Hi, Rosie. There's an idea I'd like to run past you.
I was wondering if you wouldn't mind helping me with something?
~~I hope you don't mind my asking, but are you around this weekend?~~
I'm really sorry to ask you this, but could you give me a lift home?

1 **A** <u>I hope you don't mind my asking, but are you around this weekend?</u>
  B Yes, I am. Do you need a favour?
2 **A** _____
  B What's that?
3 **A** _____
  B No, not at all. What is it?
4 **A** _____
  B Oh, don't worry about it.
5 **A** _____
  B No problem, where is it?
6 **A** _____
  B Sure, let's go.

b ▶ 06.07 Listen and check.

c Complete the conversation. Write one word in each space.

MARION Good to see you, Derek! Do you mind
            ¹_____if_____ I ask you something?
DEREK No, ²_____ at all. Go ³_____ ahead.
MARION I hope you don't mind my ⁴_____, but I was ⁵_____ if you wouldn't mind writing a few words for the club website? We're trying to get members' profiles on there.
DEREK It sounds good and I'm happy to ⁶_____. Just tell me what kind of thing you're looking at.
MARION Super, I really ⁷_____ it.
DEREK It's no ⁸_____ at all.

d ▶ 06.08 Listen and check.

2 PRONUNCIATION Sound and spelling: Consonant sounds

a ▶ 06.09 Listen and circle the correct consonant sound for the <u>underlined</u> letters.

1 I'm not <u>s</u>ure people watch as much televi<u>s</u>ion as they used to.
  <u>s</u>ure /ð/ /s/ /ʒ/ (/ʃ/) /tʃ/
  televi<u>s</u>ion /s/ /ʒ/ /ʃ/ /tʃ/ /dʒ/

2 She's also the au<u>th</u>or of a collection of <u>ch</u>ildren's books.
  au<u>th</u>or /θ/ /ð/ /ʃ/ /tʃ/
  <u>ch</u>ildren's /s/ /ʃ/ /ʒ/ /tʃ/ /dʒ/

3 There are several cau<u>s</u>es of damage to our fra<u>g</u>ile environment.
  cau<u>s</u>es /ð/ /s/ /z/ /ʒ/ /dʒ/
  fra<u>g</u>ile /ʃ/ /ʒ/ /tʃ/ /dʒ/ /tʃ/

4 I never got to know her nie<u>c</u>e very well, <u>th</u>ough.
  nie<u>c</u>e /s/ /z/ /ʃ/ /ʒ/ /tʃ/
  <u>th</u>ough /θ/ /ð/ /ʃ/ /ʒ/ /dʒ/

5 The report sugge<u>s</u>ts taking a fresh look at the heal<u>th</u> system.
  sugge<u>s</u>ts /θ/ /ʃ/ /ʒ/ /tʃ/ /dʒ/
  heal<u>th</u> /θ/ /ð/ /s/ /tʃ/ /dʒ/

6 It's an adven<u>t</u>ure story which starts with the main character in pri<u>s</u>on.
  adven<u>t</u>ure /θ/ /z/ /ʒ/ /tʃ/ /dʒ/
  pri<u>s</u>on /s/ /z/ /ʃ/ /ʒ/ /dʒ/

7 There was a lot of confu<u>s</u>ion and embarra<u>ss</u>ment when I put the question.
  confu<u>s</u>ion /s/ /z/ /ʃ/ /ʒ/ /dʒ/
  embarra<u>ss</u>ment /s/ /z/ /ʃ/ /ʒ/ /dʒ/

8 I do appre<u>c</u>iate how ur<u>g</u>ent this matter has become.
  appre<u>c</u>iate /ð/ /s/ /z/ /ʃ/ /ʒ/
  ur<u>g</u>ent /s/ /z/ /ʒ/ /tʃ/ /dʒ/

9 **A** Thanks anyway for <u>ch</u>ecking.
  B It's a plea<u>s</u>ure.
  <u>ch</u>ecking /s/ /z/ /ʒ/ /tʃ/ /dʒ/
  plea<u>s</u>ure /s/ /z/ /ʃ/ /ʒ/ /dʒ/

10 Occa<u>s</u>ionally, I have a de<u>ss</u>ert after dinner as a treat.
  Occa<u>s</u>ionally /s/ /z/ /ʃ/ /ʒ/ /dʒ/
  de<u>ss</u>ert /s/ /z/ /ʃ/ /ʒ/ /dʒ/

Nothing *beats* LAS VEGAS

1 READING

a Read the travel blog. Are the sentences true or false?

1 The bus was cheaper than other kinds of transport.
2 The journey to Vegas was not particularly interesting.
3 It takes a while for Vegas to make an impression on you.
4 The hotel wasn't one of the best in Vegas.
5 The magic show made a big impression on the writer.
6 Vegas is the last stage of their journey.

b Read the blog again and find five adjectives that mean *very good* or *very surprising*.

1 <u>amazing</u> 3 _____ 5 _____
2 _____ 4 _____

2 WRITING SKILLS
Using descriptive language

a Put the words in the correct order to make sentences.

1 through / absolutely / the journey on / quiet trails / the dark
forest was / unforgettable .
<u>The journey on quiet trails through the dark forest</u>
<u>was absolutely unforgettable.</u>

2 unbelievable, with / the scenery was / deep snow /
absolutely / high mountains in .

_____

3 absolutely / you'll find it / easy to / get to / cheap and /
mind-blowing, and it's .

_____

4 original / wooden houses / old town is / fabulous, / the /
absolutely / especially the .

_____

5 this world / absolutely / recognisable because it's / the Taj
Mahal / is instantly / out of .

_____

6 in their / we spent / cosy cottage / awesome day with
some / an absolutely / friendly villagers .

_____

I wrote 'the madness of Vegas' in my last entry, but that wasn't strong enough to describe what we found in this crazy town. We came from Lake Mead by bus, the cheapest way of getting there. That was an experience in itself because there were some amazing characters on board.

When you first come to Vegas, the sight of all those lights, massive hotels and shopping centres is absolutely awe-inspiring. We were staying in quite an ordinary hotel by Vegas standards, but it was huge. I even got lost in the lobby!

There's so much to do in Vegas: the entertainment is absolutely fabulous. We went to an aquarium, a *Star Trek* museum and a magic show, which was just mind-blowing – I think I'm starting to believe in magic now after seeing all those unbelievable tricks they do.

That was Vegas and it was really the experience of a lifetime. Our next stop is going to be somewhere a lot quieter – that won't be difficult after Vegas.

3 WRITING

a Write a travel blog about a place you've been to (different from the one you wrote about in Exercise 4 on p. 77 of the Student's Book). Use the notes to help you.

- Where you went (what kind of place is it? how did you get there? where did you stay?)
- What you did (sightseeing, entertainment, meeting people, food)
- What you saw (interesting features)
- What it was like (the good and bad points; would you recommend it?)

1 READING

a Read the article and tick (✓) the correct summary.

1. ☐ Although many people think language change is bad, it is in fact normal.
2. ☐ Language change is generally negative, and we should do our best to stop it.
3. ☐ We don't know why language change happens, but it is extremely common.

b Read the article again and tick (✓) the correct answers.

1. What does the writer say about language in small communities?
   a. ☐ Some people learn to speak better than other people.
   b. ☑ There is a lot of variation for many different reasons.

2. What point is the writer making when mentioning grandparents?
   a. ☐ That language changes over time even if people stay in the same place.
   b. ☐ That young people should learn the forms used by their grandparents.

3. Which of the following things do we learn when Jonathan Swift is mentioned?
   a. ☐ That he created a national institution to protect the English language.
   b. ☐ That, unlike in France and Italy, there was no national institution to protect the English language.

4. What positive aspect of language change does the writer mention?
   a. ☐ It allows speakers to adapt to changing situations.
   b. ☐ It helps make positive changes in society.

5. What does the writer suggest in the final sentence?
   a. ☐ Some people will always dislike how English changes.
   b. ☐ Language change in English will make speakers of English more creative.

c Write a paragraph about some ways your language, or a language you know well, varies. Remember to include:

- how differently young and old people speak the language
- how differently people from different places speak the language
- whether you like the differences or find any of them annoying.

Why does language change?

All languages change over time, and each language varies from place to place. A language may change as a result of social or political pressures. New vocabulary is often required for the latest inventions or ideas. But a language can also change for less obvious reasons.

Influences from other people

Language changes whenever speakers come into contact with each other. No two individuals speak the same way: people from different places clearly speak differently, but even within the same small community, people speak differently depending on their age, gender, origin and social and educational background. When we interact with these different speakers, in different situations, we hear new words, expressions and pronunciations, and we can make them a part of our own speech. Even if your family has lived in the same area for generations, you can probably identify a number of differences between the language you use and the way your grandparents speak or spoke. Every generation contributes to language change and when enough time has passed, the impact of these changes becomes more obvious.

Attitudes to language change

Jonathan Swift, the 18th-century Irish author, once wrote that we should find a way to stop our language changing. Even today, it is common to find this idea – some people think that language should be frozen in time and protected from fashions and social trends.

Language change is often considered a negative thing. During the 18th century, Swift and many other people felt the English language was in serious decline and that a national institution – like those that existed in France and Italy – should be created to establish rules and preserve the language. Even today, we hear people complaining about a lack of 'standards' in spoken and written English. New words and expressions, or pronunciations and changes in grammar, are criticised and are often considered bad.

Change can be a good thing

Most linguists believe that change in language, like any change in society, is unavoidable. Change is a way of keeping a language alive and useful – it gives speakers different ways of saying things with extremely small differences in meaning and ways of expressing entirely new ideas. The academies established in France and Italy have had little success in decreasing the amount of change in French or Italian, and the gradual change in opinion of Dr Johnson – a famous dictionary writer who lived at the same time as Swift – shows how ideas have developed about language change. In 1747, Johnson wrote about his desire to write a dictionary that would fix the pronunciation of English and keep it pure. But when he completed the dictionary ten years later, he admitted in his introduction that fixing a language was impossible. Like it or not, language is always changing, and English will go on doing so in many creative and – to some people – annoying ways.

Jonathan Swift

2 LISTENING

a ▶ 06.10 Listen to the podcast and tick (✓) the topics that the people mention.

	Mike	Samantha	Louise
sports			
music			
food			

b Listen again and tick (✓) the correct answers.

1 Which reason does the presenter <u>not</u> give for why people go on staycations?
   a ☐ to save money
   b ☐ to find things near where you live
   c ✓ to have a chance to do work around the house

2 What does Mike say about what made the staycation special?
   a ☐ the visits to the exhibition and the coast
   b ☐ the small changes to how he spent his day
   c ☐ the fact he wasn't staying in a hotel

3 What do we learn about Mike and his wife?
   a ☐ They don't normally eat breakfast together.
   b ☐ They always like to have a cooked breakfast.
   c ☐ They don't have a TV.

4 Which of the following statements is true about Samantha's staycation?
   a ☐ She didn't do everything she had originally planned to do.
   b ☐ She did more activity than she planned.
   c ☐ She repeated some of the activities on different days.

5 What does Samantha say about the food she ate?
   a ☐ She never ate takeaways.
   b ☐ She ate takeaways several times.
   c ☐ She only ate a takeaway once.

6 What do we learn about Louise's children during their staycation?
   a ☐ They didn't think the staycation was different from normal holidays.
   b ☐ They were unable to follow a rule Louise had made.
   c ☐ They did sport every day.

7 Which of the guests would recommend a staycation to the listeners?
   a ☐ Mike and Samantha
   b ☐ Mike and Louise
   c ☐ all three guests

c Write a blog post giving advice on taking a staycation in your country or home town. Remember to include:
   • a short definition of a staycation
   • some suggestions of places to visit
   • some suggestions of activities to do
   • ideas for people who don't have a lot of money.

◉ Review and extension

1 GRAMMAR

Tick (✓) the correct sentences. Correct the wrong sentences.

1 ☐ I recommend to visit Iguazu Falls as soon as you can.
   I recommend visiting Iguazu Falls as soon as you can.
2 ☐ Criminals should stop thinking about the consequences of their actions.
3 ☐ We're trying saving money for a new car.
4 ☐ Getting up at 6:00 in the morning is not my idea of fun.
5 ☐ The topic has been discussed on the programme last night.
6 ☐ A new ticketing system is being introduced.

2 VOCABULARY

Tick (✓) the correct sentences. Correct the wrong sentences.

1 ☐ Sally's score in the test was really impressing.
   Sally's score in the test was really impressive.
2 ☐ The film finishes with a dramatical last scene.
3 ☐ The scenery is stunning, especially on a clear day.
4 ☐ There has been a 10% increase of profits.
5 ☐ There has been a revivation of interest in photography.
6 ☐ People hardly notice the disappearing of languages.

3 WORDPOWER *out*

Complete the sentences with the words in the box. There are two extra words you do not need.

burn   chill   fall   ~~pass~~   run   stand   turn   work

1 It was such a shock that for a moment I thought I was going to ___*pass*___ out on the floor.
2 Can anybody _____ out the answer to number six?
3 We used to _____ out about really stupid things, like whose turn it was to feed the cat.
4 None of these new songs really seem to _____ out.
5 You're going to _____ out if you don't take a break soon.
6 I like to _____ out by lying on the sofa and listening to country music.

↻ REVIEW YOUR PROGRESS

Look again at Review Your Progress on p. 78 of the Student's Book. How well can you do these things now?
3 = very well   2 = well   1 = not so well

I CAN ...	
discuss choices	☐
discuss changes	☐
introduce requests and say I am grateful	☐
write a travel blog.	☐

7A | THERE'S VERY LITTLE TRAFFIC

1 GRAMMAR too / enough; so / such

a Complete the sentences with *too much*, *too many*, *enough*, *not enough*, *so* or *such*.

1 It's ___not___ big ___enough___!

2 This was _____ a good idea.

3 Have you been eating _____ _____ junk food?

4 Flights are _____ cheap now that I have six holidays a year.

5 I don't have _____ _____ vowels.

6 Paula made _____ _____ mistakes.

b Complete the text with *too much*, *too many*, *too little*, *enough*, *not enough*, *so* or *such*.

Sleep debt means you don't have [1] ___enough___ sleep. The causes are obvious – [2] _____ work and [3] _____ rest, basically – but what are the symptoms? Well, do you ever feel [4] _____ tired in the middle of the day that you can't keep your eyes open? Do you ever get [5] _____ bad headaches that you have to lie down for a while? Does this sound like you? If so, you need to do something about it. Actually, you don't need much sleep to recover from the day, but you should make sure you get [6] _____ rest – at least seven hours each day. In fact, [7] _____ sleep, more than nine hours, can be as bad as [8] _____ sleep, six hours or less. It is a good idea to have an afternoon sleep, a siesta, especially if you can't get [9] _____ hours during the night. Some people say they feel [10] _____ refreshed after a siesta that they can do twice as much. By the way, don't try not to sleep at all – people have died after [11] _____ days without sleep. Take my advice and go to bed straight away!

c ▶ 07.01 Listen and check.

2 VOCABULARY Describing life in cities

a Match 1–7 with a–g to make statements and questions.

1 [g] There is good public
2 [ ] Plans for a new motorway have upset local
3 [ ] I'm not sure that the quality of
4 [ ] But should urban
5 [ ] A familiar problem is traffic
6 [ ] You can experience air
7 [ ] Get there early because parking

a congestion at rush hour.
b development come at the cost of the environment?
c life has changed much with technology.
d pollution even in smaller towns.
e residents and they plan to protest.
f spaces are few and hard to find.
g transport, including a tram system.

b Complete the text with the expressions in the box.

air pollution   local residents   parking space
public transport   quality of life
~~traffic congestion~~   urban development

There is a lot of criticism of big cities and in many ways they are soft targets. When you're driving through a major city, the [1] _traffic congestion_ gives you a lot of time to think, as does the time spent looking for a [2] _____ , and you should consider the option of living in a village. There you would really need your car because [3] _____ is almost non-existent outside major residential areas, and nearly everything, such as the kids' schools or the supermarket, would be a drive away. Let's hope you get on well with the [4] _____ because you'll be seeing a lot of them, the same faces in the same places. Of course, with all that fresh air, the [5] _____ must be better, but at the same time you'll miss all the sights and sounds of the big city. It makes you think, doesn't it? So roll down your window, breathe in that [6] _____ and be grateful for [7] _____ .

c ▶ 07.02 Listen and check.

1 GRAMMAR Causative *have / get*

a Tick (✓) the correct sentences to match the pictures.

1. a ✓ She sent a message.
   b ☐ She had her message sent.

2. a ☐ He tied his hands.
   b ☐ He had his hands tied.

3. a ☐ She stole a car.
   b ☐ She got her car stolen.

4. a ☐ The crocodile took a tooth out.
   b ☐ The crocodile had a tooth taken out.

5. a ☐ The nurse took some blood.
   b ☐ The nurse had some blood taken.

6. a ☐ The boy ate a hot dog.
   b ☐ The boy had his hot dog eaten.

b Rewrite the sentences using the correct forms of *have* or *get*.

1. Somebody broke into our house. (get)
   Our house got broken into.

2. A photographer is taking my picture. (have)
   _____

3. They check patients' temperature twice a day. (get)
   _____

4. A man will fix my watch. (have)
   _____

5. Chocolate covered the boy's face. (get)
   _____

6. The hairdresser was cutting my hair. (get)
   _____

7. My wife's jewellery has been stolen. (have)
   _____

8. The workers had painted our fence red. (have)
   _____

9. The branches tore her jacket. (get)
   _____

10. I'm renewing my passport. (have)
    _____

2 VOCABULARY Films and TV

a Complete the text with the words in the box.

broadcast   captured   cast   editors   episode
released   script   ~~series~~   set   soundtrack

New drama

Upton Abbey, the best drama ¹___series___ British TV has to offer, returns to your screens on Monday evening with the very first ²_____ of Series 5. For those of you who don't know the background to *Upton Abbey*, most of the episodes are ³_____ in the UK, at the original Upton Abbey. All of that unique atmosphere of 1920s England is ⁴_____ on screen with a ⁵_____ of household names and a ⁶_____ written by the famous author, Peter Stokes. *Upton Abbey* is now ⁷_____ all over the world. In fact, the first four series were recently ⁸_____ on many international streaming services. To make this show appropriate for all ages, some scenes were cut by our ⁹_____ because they dealt with topics that not all viewers may be ready for. We want the whole family to watch! So on Monday, when you hear that familiar ¹⁰_____ come on, make sure you join us to watch the best drama on TV.

b ▶ 07.03 Listen and check.

3 VOCABULARY Houses

a Reorder the letters to make words.

1. a barrier between two areas of land   e n e f c   _____
2. a house with one floor   n g l o u b a w   _____
3. not joined to another house   c h d t e d a e   _____
4. a flat area outside a house   e t a c e r r   _____
5. a floor below ground level   n e a s m b e t   _____
6. a room or area under the roof   t a c t i   _____

4 PRONUNCIATION Sound and spelling: *o*

a ▶ 07.04 Listen to the story and read the audioscript on p. 68. How is the underlined letter *o* pronounced in each word in the box? Complete the table.

second   love   too   reports   ghost   most   Tower
London   poor   soldier   shouted   so   through   out

Sound 1 /ɔː/ (e.g., *four*)	Sound 2 /uː/ (e.g., *food*)
Sound 3 /ə/ (e.g., *professor*)	**Sound 4 /ʌ/ (e.g., *some*)**
Sound 5 /aʊ/ (e.g., *now*)	**Sound 6 /əʊ/ (e.g., *road*)**

7C EVERYDAY ENGLISH
We could have a table here or something

1 USEFUL LANGUAGE
Imagining how things could be

a Put the words in the correct order to make sentences.

1 plates / could / and / have / we / things here .
<u>We could have plates and things here.</u>

2 for / could / kids to / the / play / a place / be / this .

3 table / this / great / a / bedside / make / would .

4 can / barbecue / I / imagine / a / having / here .

5 there / shelves / books / be / some / for / could .

6 I / enough / can't / big / imagine / being / room / this .

7 have / done / we / professional / could / it / a / by .

8 other / would / in / room / have to / that lamp / go / the .

2 CONVERSATION SKILLS
Using vague language

a Put the words in brackets in the correct place in each sentence.

1 This could be a playroom for the twins. (kind of)
<u>This could be a kind of playroom for the twins.</u>

2 We could put our shoes in this box. (and things)

3 I can imagine this as a desk. (or something)

4 This is where all the toys, games go. (and things like that)

5 I suppose it could be a noticeboard. (sort of)

6 The small room would make a spare bedroom.
(or something like that)

7 There's a lot of junk here: old newspapers, broken toys.
(and so on)

8 Put a book under the table so it doesn't fall over.
(or something)

3 PRONUNCIATION
Stress in compound nouns

a ▶ 07.05 Listen to the sentences. <u>Underline</u> the stressed words in the compound nouns in **bold**.

1 Local residents are getting worried about the **crime rate**.
2 There's a new **shopping centre** just out of town.
3 She said the **living room** was cosy, but really, it was just small.
4 Everyone should know the threat of **climate change** by now.
5 The **police officers** are working closely with the local community.
6 We put a **solar panel** on the roof to cut energy costs.
7 Disneyland is probably the best-known **theme park**.
8 You can never find a **parking space** when you need one.
9 Pour it down the **kitchen sink** if you don't want it.
10 More could be done to help **developing nations** and build a better educational system.

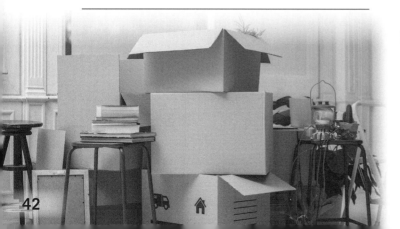

7D SKILLS FOR WRITING
There is a great deal of concern

1 READING

a Complete Amelia's email of complaint with the words in the box.

concern   least   prompt   reaction
~~regarding~~   request   residents   step

b Read the email again. Are the sentences true or false?

1 Amelia found out about this through local residents.
2 The news doesn't come as a big surprise.
3 The library has been getting less popular.
4 A journalist helped Amelia make a complaint.
5 An answer in eight days would not satisfy Amelia.
6 The council's decision is possibly illegal.

☒ ✎ ☆ ⚑   ⊗

To: Ringway Council

Subject: Closure of Ringway Library

To Whom It May Concern,

I am writing ^{1} _regarding_ the council's decision to close Ringway Library, as announced in the *Ringway Guardian* on Monday.

Among those of us who use the library on a regular basis, there is a great deal of ^{2}_____ about the impact this will have on local ^{3}_____ who need library services. The decision comes as a shock to us, particularly as statistics show that the number of people using the library rose by 20% this year.

My first ^{4}_____ was to contact the journalist at the *Ringway Guardian* who wrote the piece, and he gave me your contact details. I have tried to phone and I even visited your offices in person, but no one was available to meet me.

I believe that it is unreasonable and unfair to close the only library in the area. My ^{5}_____ is that at the very ^{6}_____ you hold a meeting to debate the issue.

If I do not hear from you within a week, my next ^{7}_____ will be to get legal advice. I am not convinced that this decision is in line with local government guidelines.

I look forward to a ^{8}_____ reply.

Best regards,

Amelia Shaw

---

2 WRITING SKILLS
Using formal language

a Are the expressions formal or informal? Tick (✓) the correct box.

		Formal	Informal
1	Thank you for your prompt response.	✓	
2	I think …		
3	I believe …		
4	The thing that really makes me angry …		
5	How about sending me a replacement?		
6	I would appreciate a replacement.		
7	Great to hear from you.		
8	Sincerely,		
9	What worries us most of all …		
10	Get back to me in a few days or …		
11	I am writing regarding …		
12	Regards,		
13	If you do not respond within three days …		
14	This is about …		

3 WRITING

a You have just found out that your local council plans to turn a children's playground near your house into a car parking area because of a lack of parking spaces. Write a formal email to complain. Use the paragraph structure and the notes to help you.

Paragraph 1: explain your reason for writing and give details (e.g., how you found out about this)

Paragraph 2: indicate why you are concerned or annoyed (e.g., children have few safe places to play)

Paragraph 3: describe what action you have taken (e.g., had a meeting with neighbours who have children)

Paragraph 4: explain what action you want the local council to take

Paragraph 5: say what action you will take if there's no response

DIY troubles

1 READING

a Read the article about DIY (Do It Yourself) – the activity of building, decorating or doing repairs yourself in your own home. Match people 1–4 with activities a–d.

1 ☐ Matt   2 ☐ Esteban   3 ☐ Sarah   4 ☐ Marina

a doing someone a favour
b doing something they thought would be easy
c fixing a problem that had existed for a long time
d trying to make something tidier

b Read the article again and tick (✓) the correct answers.

1 What do we learn from the first paragraph about the people who responded to the survey?
  a ☐ Five of them had damaged their home while doing DIY.
  b ☑ Most of them had failed to complete at least one DIY task.
  c ☐ Half of them plan to do one DIY job in the near future.

2 Why does Matt think he was lucky?
  a ☐ because he could have caused more damage to his house than he actually did
  b ☐ because he could have hurt himself more seriously than he actually did
  c ☐ because he was still able to finish his DIY work

3 What do we learn about Esteban's friend?
  a ☐ She had to pay for two separate things as a result of Esteban's accident.
  b ☐ She was partly to blame for Esteban's accident.
  c ☐ She was very angry with Esteban because she felt he had been stupid.

4 What was the original cause of Sarah's accident?
  a ☐ having to move a pile of books that was far away
  b ☐ resting her foot in an inappropriate place
  c ☐ hitting part of her body against something

5 Which of the following is **not** true about Sarah?
  a ☐ She eventually finished the DIY task.
  b ☐ She had to pay for the damage to be repaired.
  c ☐ She had a lot of cleaning work to do after the accident.

6 What does Marina suggest about the mistake that caused the accident?
  a ☐ It was caused by her laziness.
  b ☐ She probably wouldn't have made the same mistake during the daytime.
  c ☐ She was lucky the mistake didn't lead to a more serious problem than it did.

c Write a paragraph about a time you or somebody you know had a problem while trying to fix something. Remember to include:

• the task you or the person was trying to do
• whether you or the person expected it to be difficult or easy, and why
• the problem that occurred and the consequences of it.

Spring is nearly here and many people will turn their attention to DIY. But a recent survey has found that over 50% of people in the UK admit that they have at least one unfinished job to do in their home, while one in five people say they have caused damage to their home while trying to 'do it themselves.' Here's a selection of our readers' own DIY nightmares.

Matt I was doing a fairly simple task – just putting up some shelves in the cellar of my house. I was standing on a wooden table, putting a screw into the wall and suddenly I heard a bang, and the screwdriver just flew out of my hands. Then, I noticed that all the lights had gone out. I realised there was an electric cable in the wall where I was putting the screw in. I think I was lucky – I could have been badly hurt. But it wasn't all good luck – I had to have some repairs done by an electrician and it wasn't cheap.

Esteban Once, a friend of mine asked if I could help her paint some rooms in her house. I was painting one wall, standing at the top of a ladder. For some reason, at one point, I forgot I was on a ladder and I stepped to the side. Where I put my foot there was just air, and of course I lost my balance and fell off the ladder. Unfortunately, as I did this, I knocked the ladder over and spilled the paint all over the carpet. My friend was more worried about me than annoyed about my stupidity, but in the end she had to buy new carpet … and she called in professionals to do the painting!

Sarah I live in an old cottage. There's a big attic and it was a real mess – full of piles of old books, bags of clothes, everything. So I decided I would clear it all out and put in some cupboards and drawers to keep everything in order. I didn't get very far – after just a few minutes, I banged my head on the roof while I was trying to move a pile of old books. This made me jump back, and I put my right foot through the ceiling below. To try and get my balance, I stepped forward and my whole left leg went through the ceiling. It took days to clean up the mess in the rooms below and I had to get the two huge holes fixed by a professional. In the end, I decided to leave the attic messy!

Marina I had a tap that I couldn't turn off completely – there was always a bit of water coming out. I kept leaving it because I was too lazy, but one night I couldn't sleep because the sound of the water was really annoying me. So I decided to try and fix it – in the middle of the night. I tried to turn off the water supply before doing anything, but it was dark, I was half asleep and I ended up turning off the gas by mistake, instead of the water. So when I unscrewed the tap, water started spraying everywhere. I shouted so much I woke up everyone else in the house, and also the neighbours either side of us. It took a long time to clean up all the water, and we were all exhausted the next day!

2 LISTENING

a ▶ `07.06` Listen to a conversation between two friends, Sam and Julie. <u>Underline</u> the correct words to complete the sentences.

1 Sam lives *in the city centre / outside the city centre*.
2 Julie lives *in the city centre / outside the city centre*.
3 Sam and Julie are *completely / generally / not at all* satisfied with where they live.

b Listen again. Are the sentences true or false?

1 Julie wanted to use public transport to meet Sam, but it wasn't practical.
2 Sam is able to travel to the city centre from his home without difficulty.
3 Julie and Sam do not agree about how good the entertainment opportunities in the centre are.
4 Sam and Julie do not agree about the level of pollution where Julie lives.
5 Sam doesn't go to the parks in the centre because they're too far from his flat.
6 Julie is considering moving back to the city centre again.
7 Julie and Sam agree that for people living in the city centre, life is faster than for people who travel in every day.
8 Julie and Sam agree that they are both lucky to live where they live.

c Write a conversation between two people discussing the quality of life in your town. Use these questions to help you:

- How much traffic congestion is there?
- Is the public transport good? What about the parking?
- Is there much air pollution? Are there many green spaces?
- What are the entertainment opportunities?

 Review and extension

1 GRAMMAR

Tick (✓) the correct sentences. Correct the wrong sentences.

1 ☐ It was such small flat that we had to move out.
   It was such a small flat that we had to move out.
2 ☐ Don't expect too much from them.
3 ☐ I think it's already enough expensive.
4 ☐ Too many people got involved in the school play.
5 ☐ I recommend visiting the museum if there's time enough.
6 ☐ We were surprised that the kids so much enjoyed it.
7 ☐ It's a such dangerous journey just to get there.
8 ☐ I introduced myself and we had a picture took together.

2 VOCABULARY

Tick (✓) the correct sentences. Correct the wrong sentences.

1 ☐ There are not enough parkings for the office staff.
   There are not enough parking spaces for the office staff.
2 ☐ The standard of life is lower because of all the pollution.
3 ☐ People will always prefer cars to publique transport.
4 ☐ No one bothered to ask local residents how they feel.
5 ☐ The scene was cutted from the final film.
6 ☐ The next chapter in the series will be shown on Tuesday.

3 WORDPOWER *down*

Complete the sentences with a verb.

1 I was so angry, it took me a few minutes to ___*calm*___ down.
2 It's time for John to find someone nice and _____ down to start a family.
3 People will think you are arrogant if you _____ down on everyone like that.
4 You should _____ down on sweets if you want to lose weight.
5 She was offered a scholarship, but decided to _____ it down.
6 All this constant complaining is starting to _____ me down.

⟳ REVIEW YOUR PROGRESS

Look again at Review Your Progress on p. 90 of the Student's Book. How well can you do these things now?
3 = very well   2 = well   1 = not so well

I CAN ...	
discuss living in cities	☐
discuss changes to a home	☐
imagine how things could be	☐
write an email to complain.	☐

8A | I'D LIKE TO START SAVING FOR A HOME

1 GRAMMAR First and second conditionals

a Match 1–10 with a–j to make conditional sentences.

1. [f] If I stop eating out,
2. [ ] If I didn't need to work,
3. [ ] If I see Jim,
4. [ ] If the bank didn't charge such high interest,
5. [ ] If the price is too high,
6. [ ] If Sarah paid back her student loan any time soon,
7. [ ] If I feel generous,
8. [ ] If I were you,
9. [ ] If I worked for myself,
10. [ ] If we spend more on advertising,

a I could have more responsibility.
b I'd become a full-time writer.
c I'd think about what I was doing.
d I'd take out a bigger loan.
e I'll return the €20 I owe him.
f I'll save a lot of money.
g I might give some money to charity.
h I won't buy the flat.
i I'd be surprised.
j profits can increase.

b ▶ 08.01 Listen and check.

c Complete the sentences with the correct form of the verbs in brackets. Use contractions where possible.

1. If the weather ___is___ (be) nice again tomorrow, I ___'ll go___ (go) for a walk.
2. If money _____ (grow) on trees, inflation _____ (be) very high.
3. I _____ (make) the coffee if you _____ (do) the eggs.
4. I _____ (go) to Ancient Greece if I _____ (can travel) back in time.
5. If I _____ (be) you, I _____ (tell) the truth.
6. If I _____ (can't find) my blue tie, I _____ (wear) the red one instead.
7. So _____ (take) a taxi if you _____ (be) in a hurry.
8. If today _____ (be) Saturday, I _____ (stay) in bed for a couple more hours.
9. I _____ (become) a doctor if I _____ (have) a chance to start all over again.
10. Don't worry. If I _____ (feel) bad, I _____ (give) you a call.

2 VOCABULARY Money and finance

a Complete the sentences with the missing words. The first letters are given for you.

1. It's a good idea to put aside some s_____ for the future.
2. We will d_____ your account the annual cost of the credit card.
3. We planned €1,500 for renovation in our b_____, but in the end it cost much more than that.
4. She's very wealthy, but she donates a lot to c_____ and other good causes.
5. Government borrowing has led to the massive national d_____.
6. The research council agreed to a _____ a grant for the project.
7. Buying your own house is a good i_____ while property prices are low.
8. After Hurricane Harry, generous d_____ are coming in from all over the world.
9. George's annual i_____ is now €70,000 with his new pay rise – but that's before tax.

b Complete the text with the words in the box.

| aside | budget | debit | debt | donations | finance |
| grant | income | investment | ~~living~~ | pay | rate |

John Roberts made a [1] ___living___ as a fisherman working for a big fishing company. However, John always wanted to have his own boat and business, so he put [2]_____ savings for years, and when the interest [3]_____ was low, he went to a bank. The bank checked the [4]_____ which John had prepared showing sales vs. costs and then agreed to [5]_____ the project. This meant John now had a very large [6]_____, but he considered the boat as a sound [7]_____. Unfortunately, business became more difficult because of overfishing and environmental damage. John's [8]_____ dropped lower and lower and he was struggling just to [9]_____ off the interest on his loan. Before long, the bank was starting to [10]_____ his account with penalties for missed payments. John was desperate and he wrote about his situation on a website for start-up companies. This worked. The local council immediately awarded John a [11]_____ and [12]_____ came in from people in the area. Thanks to this, John's business survived.

c ▶ 08.02 Listen and check.

8B I WOULD HAVE TOLD THE MANAGER

1 GRAMMAR Third conditional; *should have* + past participle

a Put the words in the correct order to make sentences.

1 had / would / if that / have / called the police / happened / to me, I .
   If that had happened to me, I would have called the police.

2 had / realised if / her bag / someone / she would / have / taken .
   _____

3 been all right / if / have / got there / more quickly, everything / might / I could / have .
   _____

4 if / find / the safe / they'd been / would / have / brighter, they / tried to .
   _____

5 Jack / hadn't / them / wouldn't / know / I / her if / introduced .
   _____

6 changed / if / ages ago / I / you, I / have / the locks / were / would .
   _____

7 she / her neighbour / hadn't / have / been / for hours if / could / come round / lying there .
   _____

8 you / in / shouldn't / bag / have / your valuables / one / put all .
   _____

9 to prison / the judge / for / a lot longer / should / him / have / sent .
   _____

10 you / what / was / watching / should / been / have / happening .
   _____

b Underline the correct words to complete the statements and questions.

1 Things would have been even worse if I *haven't listened* / *hadn't listened* to you.
2 If she had contacted me, I *would have* / *would have been* helped her.
3 What *would* / *should* you have done if they hadn't arrived?
4 I would have become the manager if I *have been* / *had been* working there as long as you.
5 If the train hadn't been late, I *can get* / *might have got* there on time.
6 *Would you pay* / *Had you paid* €100 if you could see the questions before the exam?
7 If you hadn't dropped your laptop, it would still *work* / *have worked*.
8 You *would* / *should* have helped if you wanted us to clean up the kitchen quickly.
9 I'm sorry. I *shouldn't* / *wouldn't* have been so rude.
10 I don't understand why Carolina said that. *Would* / *Should* you have reacted in the same way?

2 VOCABULARY Crime

a Look at the pictures. Complete the sentences with the words in the box. There are two extra words you do not need.

bribery ~~burglar~~ judge jury
kidnapper robber shoplifting suspect

1 The __burglar__ didn't realise there was a cat at home.

2 The police caught the _____ still in the bank.

3 It was Lisa's first experience _____ .

4 The _____ brought back the baby when it started crying.

5 The _____ didn't find the court case very interesting.

6 Does this count as a present or is this _____ ?

b Underline the correct words to complete the text.

One night I came home very late and I couldn't find my keys, so I had to break [1]*into* / *through* my own house! I was climbing through a window when a woman on the street shouted, 'Police! There's a [2]*burglary* / *murder*!' I got down and explained that it was my house and I wasn't a [3]*cheat* / *burglar*, but she called me a [4]*liar* / *judge*. She said that she was a [5]*robber* / *witness* and that she would give [6]*evidence* / *verdict* when I was accused [7]*in* / *of* breaking and entering. She would happily come to the [8]*trial* / *case* at [9]*prison* / *court* to testify against me. She was really excited now and went on that the [10]*judge* / *jury* would find me [11]*guilty* / *innocent*, and the [12]*judge* / *jury* would give me a very long prison [13]*sentence* / *arrest*. I'd have to go to a horrible prison where the prisoners [14]*murder* / *lie* to one another and [15]*steal* / *burgle* their cellmates' food just to survive. She was out of breath now and just about to start again when suddenly my house keys fell out of my back pocket. I wished her goodnight and went inside the house.

c ▶ 08.03 Listen and check.

3 PRONUNCIATION Stressed and unstressed words

a ▶ 08.04 Listen and underline the stressed words in each sentence.

1 It should have been sent on Tuesday.
2 If I had seen her, I would have shouted.
3 If you had told me, it could have been different.
4 We'd never have known if she had stayed at home.
5 They shouldn't have thrown it away.
6 She shouldn't have taken my purse.

8C EVERYDAY ENGLISH
You'll find somewhere

1 USEFUL LANGUAGE
Being encouraging

a Tick (✓) the most encouraging response.

1 We'll never be able to afford it.
  a ☐ You're probably right.
  b ✓ Don't give up hope.
  c ☐ That's a fair point.

2 I'll never see her again.
  a ☐ I'm sure you will.
  b ☐ That's very possible.
  c ☐ Not in a million years!

3 It started to go wrong right from the start.
  a ☐ That's life.
  b ☐ What did you expect?
  c ☐ It might work out fine.

4 That's another opportunity lost.
  a ☐ There'll be plenty more, don't worry.
  b ☐ I'd start worrying if I were you.
  c ☐ I agree with you there, and I'd be really worried.

5 I'm really worried about this interview.
  a ☐ I'm sure it'll be fine.
  b ☐ There's no time for that.
  c ☐ How can you be so sure?

6 There's not much chance of it working.
  a ☐ There would have been if it weren't for you.
  b ☐ You never know. We might pull it off.
  c ☐ No – thanks to you. We won't try it again.

b ▶ 08.05 Listen and check.

2 CONVERSATION SKILLS Showing you have things in common

a <u>Underline</u> the correct words to complete one side of a telephone conversation.

> Really sorry to hear about your car. The ¹*same / similar / like* thing happened to me a couple of years ago. My car was stolen right outside my house, and believe it or not, I've just had a ²*same / similar / like* experience. I had my purse stolen from my bag when I was in the queue in the supermarket. ... You don't surprise me. It was just ³*as / like* that when I called the insurance company. They kept me waiting for ages, so I know the ⁴*experience / feeling*. ... It was the same ⁵*with / to / by* me. What can you do? ... True, that's just like ⁶*that / as / when* Sarah's flat was burgled. I don't know what things are coming to.

b ▶ 08.06 Listen and check.

3 PRONUNCIATION Word groups

a ▶ 08.07 Listen to the sentences from a telephone conversation. Mark one pause (//) in the correct place in each sentence.

1 Hello, // this is John Peters.
2 It's Simon again from NatEast Bank.
3 It's 973 412.
4 No, but thanks anyway.
5 Do you want to pay by cash or by credit card?
6 That's fine, no worries.
7 I'm sorry, but I didn't get that.
8 All the best and speak to you soon.
9 Goodbye, thanks for calling.

If you love classic cinema, you can't do better than the original 1933 *King Kong*, one of the most famous adventure films ever made. One of the things I love about it is that you can watch it again and again and still feel the same drama and excitement.

The story is an interesting variation on the *Beauty and the Beast* theme, with the beast being a huge ape that is captured on an exotic island and transported to the USA. The 'beauty' in the film is the woman used to trick the ape. The drama really begins when the ape escapes in the USA and goes to look for the woman …

What makes this a brilliant film, both now and then, is the story – it keeps you guessing all the way through, going from the jungle to skyscrapers. The acting is also excellent, and you even start feeling sorry for the ape!

King Kong is a hugely entertaining film for viewers of all ages and I highly recommend it if you want to escape for a couple of hours. It might be an old film, but it is much more powerful than the remakes and it is a real classic.

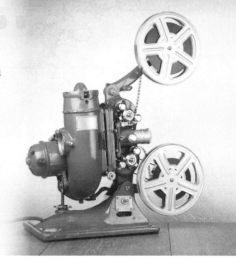

1 READING

a Read the review and tick (✓) the questions that the review answers.

1 ☑ What kind of film is it?
2 ☐ Did it win any awards?
3 ☐ Is it based on a book?
4 ☐ Where does the action happen?
5 ☐ What happens at the end?
6 ☐ Is it suitable for teenagers?
7 ☐ Have there been more recent versions of the film?
8 ☐ Does the reviewer recommend it?

b Read the article again. Are the sentences true or false?

1 The reviewer has just seen *King Kong* for the first time.
2 The reviewer describes an early inspiration for the film.
3 According to the review, the most exciting part of the film takes place on the exotic island.
4 The plot of the film is completely predictable.
5 According to the reviewer, the film has an emotional impact on the viewer.
6 *King Kong* is ideal to watch with the whole family.

2 WRITING SKILLS Organising a review

a Read the sentences and decide if they are suitable for a review of a film or book. Tick (✓) the correct box.

3 WRITING

a Write a review of a film you enjoyed (or hated). You could get information online and, even better, watch the film again in English. Use the paragraph structure and the notes to help you.

> Paragraph 1: Introduce the film and explain why you have chosen it
>
> Paragraph 2: Outline the plot and introduce the main characters
>
> Paragraph 3: Outline the key strengths of the film
>
> Paragraph 4: Summarise the review and give your final opinion

	Suitable	Not suitable
1 This is really a children's book, but I am sure that many adults would enjoy it, too.	✓	
2 It's better to stream the film so you can watch it in the comfort of your own home.		
3 The lead actor, Joshua Samson, was born in a small Australian town, but moved to Hollywood.		
4 There are a lot of cooking programmes on TV, but this is easily the best.		
5 Believe it or not, the film was so frightening that I couldn't sleep after I watched it.		
6 I bought this book on a fantastic holiday I had in Greece two summers ago.		
7 There is a lot of difficult vocabulary and this makes it hard to read.		
8 To find out what happens at the end, you'll have to watch it yourself!		

1 READING

a Read the article about four tools that can be used to help you manage your money. Tick (✓) the correct boxes.

	MoneyHealth	MoneyWorker	MoneyGarden	CheckMyMoney
Totally free				
Works offline				
Works on multiple devices				

Four great
financial tools

Managing your money and keeping to a budget can be difficult, but there are some fantastic personal finance tools that can make our lives much easier. Here are some of the best, perfect for keeping track of your finances.

MoneyHealth

MoneyHealth instantly lets you see how healthy your finances are. It connects to your bank accounts (although at the moment, it only works with bank accounts in the UK) and keeps track of how much money is in each account and where your money is going. But the strength of this tool is that it does much more. It also lets you create a family budget, helps you set up goals for your savings and even 'learns' what kinds of things you're spending your money on. MoneyHealth also suggests products that might be of interest, like credit cards that could save you money. The only thing it doesn't do is actually move your money around or make payments. Its function is just to describe your financial situation. Unfortunately, it's an expensive program, especially because it only works on one device.

MoneyGarden

This tool allows you to link up to almost 200 banks and other financial institutions. It produces graphs and other reports so you can see clearly when you spend your money and on what. Its application has won awards for its practical design, but like the computer program, it does need an Internet connection to be useful. The program is free, but you can choose to make a donation to the creators if you find it useful.

MoneyWorker

This is an app that connects to all your devices. It keeps track of your financial transactions, such as when you use your credit card or when your bank account is debited. It also helps you create an easy-to-use budget and set financial goals. The program runs on your computer, tablet or phone, and you have access to your financial information even if you're not connected to the Internet. But what makes MoneyWorker different is the fact that you don't just get access to software to help you manage your money – you also join a community of users around the world who can answer your finance questions and share ideas. Although this is expensive, you can try it out for free for one month.

CheckMyMoney

This is a financial tool with one main job – to create a budget for you. Once you enter the details of your bank accounts, it analyses the data and creates a plan with a budget and suggestions for how to save money and cut your spending. Once you've set up your budget, the program helps you keep to it. The basic version of CheckMyMoney is totally free to use. However, if you want to use the added features on the app, or if you want to be able to link up more than two bank accounts, you have to pay a one-time fee to upgrade to the premium version. Users report the app can be slow when you're not connected to the Internet.

b Read the article again. Are the sentences true or false?

1 MoneyHealth can be used by people all over the world.
2 MoneyHealth isn't able to make any changes to your bank accounts.
3 MoneyWorker gives you a way of asking other people for advice about money.
4 You can use MoneyWorker for a period of time without paying.
5 MoneyGarden offers you a way to check your finances visually.
6 MoneyGarden is not suitable for people who want to check their finances while travelling.
7 CheckMyMoney can help you reduce how much you spend.
8 CheckMyMoney does not work at all unless you pay a yearly fee.

c Write a paragraph about how you manage your money. Remember to include:

- whether you are able to put aside savings regularly
- if you make a budget every week, month or year
- if you ask anybody for advice about managing money.

2 LISTENING

a ▶ 08.08 Listen to a radio programme about local crimes. Put the events in the order they happened.

- ☐ burglaries
- ☐ a successful arrest
- ☐ a robbery in a shop
- ☐ shoplifting

b Listen to the programme again and tick (✓) the correct answers.

1 Which of the following statements is true about calling the programme to give information?
   a ☐ You need to give your name.
   b ✓ You may earn money if the information is useful.
   c ☐ The first person you speak to when you call is a police officer.

2 What is suggested about the two men who came in the shop in Rhona Kent's report?
   a ☐ They were both probably involved in the robbery.
   b ☐ The first man didn't realise what the second man was doing.
   c ☐ They left the shop at the same time.

3 What do we learn about the theft at the electronics shop?
   a ☐ Nobody in the shop knew about it.
   b ☐ The thief attacked a young woman.
   c ☐ It happened at night.

4 What does Inspector Jones say when talking about the burglaries?
   a ☐ The burglars took as much jewellery as they did electrical items.
   b ☐ Some of the burglaries could have been avoided.
   c ☐ The burglaries have happened in houses far apart from each other.

5 What does the presenter say about the criminals responsible for a crime previously discussed on the programme?
   a ☐ No one has gone to prison.
   b ☐ Listeners helped the police identify them.
   c ☐ Some of the crimes still haven't been solved.

c Think about a crime that you have heard or read about recently. Write a short conversation between two people discussing it. Use these questions to help you:

- What was the crime?
- How did they hear about it?
- What happened?
- Did the police catch the criminal? Are they looking for them now?

◉ Review and extension

1 GRAMMAR

Tick (✓) the correct sentences. Correct the wrong sentences.

1 ☐ Before you listen to my instructions, everything will be fine.
   If you listen to my instructions, everything will be fine.
2 ☐ I'd be amazed if she had more children.
3 ☐ It would be a great idea that everyone cycled to work.
4 ☐ Tracy would tell me if she were unhappy about it.
5 ☐ It could be nice if there were more people like her.
6 ☐ It was fantastic if you had come with us.

2 VOCABULARY

Tick (✓) the correct sentences. Correct the wrong sentences.

1 ✓ It's difficult to make a living as a professional dancer.
2 ☐ One area where saving could be made is transport.
3 ☐ The income from tourism could be much higher.
4 ☐ I'm not sure that our budjet is big enough for this.
5 ☐ There has been a large increase in donations to charities.
6 ☐ The main suspect was not the murder but someone else.
7 ☐ A man has been sentenced and will appear in court later.
8 ☐ The theif was arrested when she tried to burgle a flat.

3 WORDPOWER *take*

Complete the text with the words in the box.

~~charge~~ granted it pleasure seriously word

My wife goes out to work and I look after our children. It made sense after her promotion, and I was happy to take ¹ _charge_ . But take my ² _____ for it – staying at home with the kids is harder than I imagined. Of course, they're my kids and I take real ³ _____ in seeing them grow up, but they need a lot of attention. When I came home from work, I took it for ⁴ _____ that they were fed, clothed and entertained, but now I have to do all that. I take my new role ⁵ _____, but there are days when I think I can't take ⁶ _____ any longer!

◉ REVIEW YOUR PROGRESS

Look again at Review Your Progress on p. 102 of the Student's Book. How well can you do these things now?
3 = very well   2 = well   1 = not so well

I CAN ...	
discuss personal finance	☐
discuss moral dilemmas and crime	☐
be encouraging	☐
write a review.	☐

9A WHAT REALLY SHOCKS ME IS THAT IT COSTS €250,000

1 GRAMMAR Relative clauses

a Match 1–10 to a–j to make sentences.

1 [d] Medicine is one of those professions
2 [ ] Even today there are still diseases
3 [ ] There is research into 3D printers
4 [ ] Paramedics are basically staff
5 [ ] There may come a day
6 [ ] These tablets are for patients
7 [ ] My first job was as a nurse at a private school,
8 [ ] Doctors don't have a lot of sympathy for those
9 [ ] There is medicine for an upset stomach
10 [ ] I told her to see Dr Brown,

a that could create body parts for transplants.
b that you can buy in any chemist's.
c when machines can make blood for patients.
d where you can make a real difference.
e that there is no known cure for.
f which was an interesting experience.
g who is a specialist in eye surgery.
h who won't help themselves.
i who work alongside nurses and doctors.
j whose temperatures go higher than 39 degrees.

b Underline the correct words to complete the text. If no word is needed, choose Ø.

We like to think that we live in a world ¹that / where / which everyone has access to professional medical care ²Ø / who / that can take care of their needs. Unfortunately, for those ³who / Ø / which live in the developing world, ⁴Ø / which / that is about 85% of the Earth's population, this is far from the case. Too often either the treatment from trained professionals ⁵who / which / what they need is impossible to get, or it costs money ⁶which / what / who they don't have. People ⁷which / Ø / who need treatment then often have to look for alternatives ⁸that / whose / what are relatively cheap and available.

There is a long tradition of using natural medicine, for example, plants ⁹which / where / whose leaves and flowers can be used to take away pain. However, natural medicine is of limited use in situations ¹⁰where / that / Ø the patient is very ill. Even so, there are people ¹¹who / which / Ø suffer from serious diseases ¹²who / Ø / which trust natural medicine more than modern methods. This may sound crazy to Westerners ¹³who / Ø / which have the luxury of professional help, but people ¹⁴which / that / Ø believe in this kind of treatment strongly enough might benefit just from the psychological effect, ¹⁵which / that / Ø could mean the difference between life and death.

c ▶09.01 Listen and check.

2 VOCABULARY Health

a Underline the correct words to complete the sentences.

1 The best way to _cure_ / heal / develop a cold is to rest and drink plenty of liquids.
2 I can't play on Saturday because I'm still caring for / getting over / treating the flu.
3 My throat and chest feel really sore. I must have some kind of bruise / cough / infection.
4 Tim's got a fever. He says he feels hot and cold, and his face is really bruised / dizzy / pale.
5 She bumped / coughed / sneezed to get his attention.
6 I've got a big infection / strain / scar on my knee from when I fell off the ladder.

b Complete the text with the words in the box.

| ached | bruise | ~~bumped~~ | develop | dizzy |
| get over | pass out | shiver | strained | treat |

It all started when I was jogging in the park. I ¹ _bumped_ into something, fell over and got a big ² _____ on my leg. It ³ _____ a bit. I was worried I had ⁴ _____ my leg as it wasn't comfortable. I thought it was best to do something about it, so I looked up some advice on the Internet and decided to ⁵ _____ myself.

There was a lot of information, all quite confusing, but I found a recipe for a special sports drink and drank a couple of litres of it. About an hour later, it hit me. I felt ⁶ _____, my head was going round and round and I started to ⁷ _____ – I couldn't hold a cup in my hands. I thought I was going to ⁸ _____, but I managed to crawl into bed. A week later, I'm beginning to ⁹ _____ it and thank goodness I didn't ¹⁰ _____ any complications. I won't be using any of those Internet sites again, though.

c ▶09.02 Listen and check.

3 PRONUNCIATION Sound and spelling: *ui*

a ▶09.03 Listen to the sentences and read the audioscript on p. 75. How are the underlined letters *ui* pronounced in each word in the box? Complete the table.

| ~~bruise~~ | quite | bodybuilder | nuisance |
| fruit | suits | guilty | enquire | biscuit |

Sound 1 /ɪ/ (e.g., *hit*)	Sound 2 /uː/ (e.g., *food*)	Sound 3 /aɪ/ (e.g., *time*)
	bruise	

9B | THEY HAD NO IDEA IT WAS A FRAUD

1 GRAMMAR
Reported speech; reporting verbs

a Read the newspaper headlines and <u>underline</u> the correct words to complete the text.

> **EXCLUSIVE! Robins did NOT walk around the world!**
>
> **HOW DID ROBINS DO THE WALK SO QUICKLY?**
>
> **Tell us the truth!**　**ROBINS: 'No comment!'**
>
> **Robins: 'You just want a good story!'**
>
> **Robins: 'I HAVE NOTHING TO HIDE!'**　**EXCLUSIVE! ROBINS USED A PRIVATE PLANE!**
>
> **Robins: 'I only flew a short way'**　**Robins: 'I'll give you your money back'**
>
> **WE'VE BEEN CHEATED!**
>
> **Police won't take legal action**
>
> **POLICE TELL ROBINS TO TELL THE TRUTH**

Simon Robins was a hero when he walked around the world to raise money for charity, but journalists have now discovered ¹*that he didn't do* / *him not doing* it. Actually, Robins flew most of the way. Journalists wondered ²*how had he* / *how he had* done the walk so quickly and asked ³*him to explain* / *that he explained*. At first, Robins refused ⁴*to talk* / *talking* about it, complaining ⁵*that the press wanted* / *the press wanting* just to get a good story, and completely denied ⁶*to have* / *having* anything to hide. However, journalists found out ⁷*he had used* / *him using* a private plane and finally Robins admitted ⁸*to fly* / *flying* for part of the long journey. Robins insisted ⁹*he had walked* / *to have walked* a lot of the way and promised ¹⁰*to give* / *giving* money back to people who believed ¹¹*they had been* / *having been* cheated. The police have informed ¹²*that* / *us that* they won't be taking legal action against Robins, but they have ordered ¹³*that he give* / *him to give* a full and correct account of his 'walk' around the world.

b ▶ 09.04 Listen and check.

c Complete the reported speech sentences. Use contractions where possible.

1 'I'm staying at home with my sister.'
   Brian said <u>he was staying at home with his sister</u>.

2 'It took three hours to get there.'
   Jenny told me that _____.

3 'It may be a problem.'
   The nurse thought that _____.

4 'Who are you going with?'
   My mum asked me _____.

5 'Why didn't you tell me?'
   Samuel wanted to know _____.

6 'I'm sorry I broke the vase.'
   I apologised _____.

7 'Please be on time, everyone.'
   The boss reminded _____.

2 VOCABULARY Verbs describing thought and knowledge

a <u>Underline</u> the correct words to complete the sentences.

1 'I don't understand why we can't see our doctor this week. He must be on holiday.'
   Elena *had no idea* / *reminded* / <u>*assumed*</u> that her doctor was on holiday.

2 'After reading his book, I decided I didn't like his writing style.'
   José *came to the conclusion* / *promised* / *suspected* that he didn't like that author.

3 'I've never heard of the Spanish Flu.'
   James *assumed* / *suspected* / *had no idea* what the Spanish Flu was.

4 'We think the waiter is stealing money from that restaurant.'
   They *asked* / *agreed* / *suspected* the waiter was stealing money.

5 'I'm so lucky to have met Pamela.'
   He *agreed* / *realised* / *told* how lucky he was to be with Pamela.

6 'You're going to pay, aren't you, darling?'
   My husband *promised* / *assumed* / *reminded* I was going to pay.

b Complete the words in the sentences.

1 Gosh, I never r<u>e a l i s e d</u> how difficult it would be to get everyone to agree.

2 The government has no i_ _ _ that he hasn't paid tax in years.

3 Who do you s _ _ _ _ _ stole the information from the company's database?

4 I can only c_ _ _ to the conclusion that you are no longer interested in the job.

5 Zelda hasn't been to training for weeks, so I a_ _ _ _ she's left.

9C EVERYDAY ENGLISH
What's the big secret?

1 USEFUL LANGUAGE
Expressing uncertainty

a Put the conversation in the correct order.

- [ ] **B** I've really no idea. What on earth are you talking about?
- [ ] **A** Oh, come on! Black Street, you must remember.
- [ ] **A** The Black Street Café. We worked there one summer.
- [ ] **B** Sorry, but I've no idea who you are.
- [ ] **A** It's Tim, from Black Street.
- [ ] **B** Oh, Tim! What on earth are you doing here?
- [1] **A** Hi! Do you recognise me?
- [ ] **A** I wanted to ask you the same question.
- [ ] **B** Black Street? I haven't got a clue where that is.

b ▶09.05 Listen and check.

2 CONVERSATION SKILLS
Clarifying a misunderstanding

a Complete the conversation. Write one word in each gap.

A Here's your room. Have a nice stay.

B Er, I understood ¹___that___ we booked a large room.

A It *is* large – you should see the small rooms.

B And did I ²_____ this wrong? I thought there was a sea view.

A The sea is terrible. You don't want to see it.

B There's not even a shower!

A Have I ³_____ something? I ⁴_____ you were on holiday. You'll be outside most of the time.

B But ⁵_____ you say this was a luxury hotel?

A It used to be – 20 years ago!

b ▶09.06 Listen and check.

3 PRONUNCIATION
Linking and intrusion

a Write the correct linking sounds that are added in the <u>underlined</u> phrases: /j/, /r/ or /w/.

1. I met John in the town centre <u>the other</u> day.   _/j/_
2. Would you know <u>where I</u> could find a post office?   _____
3. I can't afford it. It's <u>too expensive</u>.   _____
4. That's the phone. Could you <u>answer it</u>, please?   _____
5. Don't leave the window open when you <u>go out</u>.   _____
6. Can you <u>play a</u> piece for us on the piano?   _____
7. Don't assume <u>I earn</u> a lot of money from doing this.   _____
8. There is a new trade agreement between <u>Russia and</u> France.   _____
9. If it's <u>so important</u> to you, you can have mine.   _____
10. I do think <u>she ought</u> to explain exactly what she did.   _____

b ▶09.07 Listen and check.

9D | SKILLS FOR WRITING
People argue that it is no use at all

Keeping sport healthy

The conventional opinion about sport is that it has a positive influence on individuals' physical condition. However, some people claim that there are negative aspects of sport that should make us examine its contribution more closely.

It is said that there are several good reasons for doing sport. First, fitness is connected to health, and doing sport helps you to keep fit and stay active. Second, we usually do sport with other people, and social interaction helps people stay mentally healthy and happy.

One argument given against sport is that it puts stress on the body. Aside from extreme sports, even everyday activities like running can be harmful if you do them too much. Some people also worry about the long-term effects of various drugs and sports supplements.

Furthermore, it is claimed that the competitive element of sport, the 'win at all costs' mentality, can make people aggressive. The reasoning is that, in this case, sport becomes all about winning rather than being healthy and enjoying what you do.

In conclusion, I believe that doing sport can be a healthy and fun way to spend time if it is done in moderation and with the right spirit. The benefits of a healthy lifestyle almost certainly outweigh the disadvantages.

1 READING

a Read the essay about the value of sport in keeping people healthy and in shape. Are the sentences true or false?

1 Most people think that sport is a good thing.
2 The writer gives two reasons why sport is worthwhile.
3 Running is an example of an extreme sport.
4 Drugs only have an immediate effect on the body.
5 We should try to be the best at whatever sport we do.
6 The conclusion says that it is good to do some sport.

b Read the essay again and tick (✓) the correct words to complete the sentences.

1 In the first paragraph, the writer ... .
   a ✓ outlines the issue
   b ☐ summarises the issue
   c ☐ criticises the issue
2 In the next three paragraphs, the writer presents ... .
   a ☐ the results of some research
   b ☐ their own opinion
   c ☐ different arguments
3 A key argument in the second paragraph is that sport ... .
   a ☐ is the most effective way of staying fit
   b ☐ builds good relationships
   c ☐ is as much about mental as physical health
4 The third paragraph uses drugs as an example of ... .
   a ☐ an unknown factor
   b ☐ something necessary to reduce stress levels
   c ☐ something used too much in sport
5 The main idea in the fourth paragraph is that ... .
   a ☐ professional sport is a bad example for people
   b ☐ when you do sport, it is natural to want to win
   c ☐ the main purpose of sport should not be beating others
6 In the conclusion, the writer ... .
   a ☐ gives their personal opinion
   b ☐ introduces the strongest argument
   c ☐ presents a unique way of looking at the issue

2 WRITING SKILLS
Presenting a series of arguments

a Complete the sentences with the words in the box.

> addition   against   ~~argue~~   conclude
> important   spite   suggests   unlike

1 People often _____argue_____ that drug companies are too greedy.
2 This _____ that most people are unaware of the problem.
3 One argument _____ private healthcare is that it excludes some people.
4 In _____, there may not be enough doctors to help everyone.
5 To _____, both sides of the argument have some validity.
6 It's _____ not to forget that this medicine is not available everywhere.
7 In _____ of advances in medicine, we have no cure for many diseases.
8 We can eat fresh fruit all year round now, _____ 50 years ago.

3 WRITING

a Write an essay on the topic 'Are we healthier today than we were 100 years ago?' Use the paragraph structure and the notes to help you.

- Introduction: outline the topic
- Main argument for better health: medicine and technology, better nutrition is available
- Other arguments for: more leisure time
- Arguments against: bad diets, cars, TV and computers, life moves too fast
- Conclusion: summarise the arguments and give your opinion

Georges Méliès

1 READING

a Read the article about Georges Méliès.
Put the events in the order they happened.

- [ ] He bought a theatre.
- [ ] He developed new filmmaking techniques.
- [ ] He lived abroad.
- [ ] He made his own camera.
- [ ] He received a prize from his country.
- [ ] He saw his first film.
- [ ] He stopped making films.

b Read the article again and tick (✓) the correct answers.

1 Méliès went to study in London … .
   - a [ ] because there was a very famous art school there
   - b [✓] because of his parents' wishes
   - c [ ] because he wanted to learn more about theatre magic

2 After buying the Théâtre Robert-Houdin, … .
   - a [ ] Méliès performed shows there using things he learned in London
   - b [ ] Méliès split his time between working there and continuing his studies
   - c [ ] Méliès was able to save up a lot of money from the profits

3 After seeing the Lumière brothers' film, Méliès … .
   - a [ ] suggested they collaborate on a project together
   - b [ ] introduced them to a filmmaker in London
   - c [ ] made them an offer that they did not accept

4 Méliès started to make his own films … .
   - a [ ] after he was given a camera from Robert Paul
   - b [ ] using a camera he made himself
   - c [ ] after learning some techniques from Robert Paul

5 Méliès's decision to start experimenting with special effects … .
   - a [ ] was the result of an accidental discovery
   - b [ ] came after he felt unable to film a street scene in the way he wanted
   - c [ ] was made because he felt that other films he'd watched were unsatisfactory

6 The writer suggests Méliès stopped making films … .
   - a [ ] because audiences stopped going to see them
   - b [ ] because he didn't find the work interesting any more
   - c [ ] because he wanted to work in the theatre again

7 When he was older, Méliès … .
   - a [ ] was totally forgotten in France
   - b [ ] returned to making films
   - c [ ] did not have to pay for his own accommodation

c Write a paragraph about someone famous in your country who only became well known later in their life. Remember to include:

- what the person is famous for
- what they did before finding fame
- what your opinion is of this person.

The Oscar-winning film *Hugo* by Martin Scorsese has people around the world interested in a French director born over 150 years ago. Marie-Georges-Jean Méliès was born in Paris in 1861. From an early age, he showed a particular interest in the arts. After studying at a famous art school in Paris, Méliès continued his studies in London – his parents insisted he learn English. While in London, he developed an interest in theatre magic.

When he returned to Paris, he worked at his father's factory and took over as manager when his father retired. His position meant that he was able to save enough money to buy the famous Théâtre Robert-Houdin when it was put up for sale in 1888. From that point on, Méliès worked full time, performing shows at the theatre, using techniques that he studied while in London, as well as working on his own tricks.

When the Lumière brothers – said to be the first-ever filmmakers – showed their film to the public for the first time, Méliès was a member of the audience. What he witnessed clearly had a strong effect upon him. After the show, he asked the Lumière brothers if he could buy their projector, but they turned him down. However, Méliès had come to the conclusion that filmmaking was his future, so he went to meet Robert Paul – a British filmmaker – in London. Méliès looked at Paul's camera-projector and built his own soon afterwards. Within months, Méliès was making and showing his own films.

In the autumn of 1896, an event occurred that changed the way Méliès looked at filmmaking. While filming a simple street scene, Méliès's camera got stuck and it took him a few seconds to solve the problem. When he later watched the film, Méliès was amazed by the effect that the incident had on what he'd filmed – objects suddenly appeared, disappeared or were transformed into other objects. It occurred to him that he could use techniques like this to change the appearance of time and space in his films. He used this discovery to create complex special effects.

Méliès made a wide range of films. He is most famous for his fantasy films, but he also made advertising films and serious dramas. However, after a while, audiences stopped finding his work so interesting or unusual, and in 1912, he gave up making films. In 1915, he was forced to turn his film studio into a theatre and he started presenting live shows again. In 1923, he ran out of money and his theatre was knocked down. Méliès was almost totally forgotten, but in the late 1920s, his contribution to cinema was recognised by the French and he was given a special award – the Legion of Honour – and a rent-free flat where he would live for the rest of his life.

Georges Méliès died in 1938 after making over 500 films. He paid for, produced and starred in almost every one.

2 LISTENING

a ▶ 09.08 Listen to a conversation between a doctor and a patient. Match the three things the patient asks about 1–3 with the advice the doctor gives a–c.

1 ☐ cough
2 ☐ injuries from a bike accident
3 ☐ injections for a trip abroad

a Speak to somebody else.
b Come back if the problem doesn't go away.
c Use some medicine.

b Listen again and tick (✓) the correct answers.

1 How long has the patient had his cough?
   a ☐ for two days
   b ✓ for four days
   c ☐ for a few weeks

2 What does the doctor say about the patient's cold?
   a ☐ It will probably go away on its own.
   b ☐ It will probably cause a chest infection later.
   c ☐ It may be caused by having several colds at the same time.

3 What does the doctor say about the patient's bike accident?
   a ☐ The patient probably wasn't seriously injured since he didn't pass out.
   b ☐ The patient did not do the right thing after having the accident.
   c ☐ The patient should go to hospital now for further checks.

4 What does the doctor say the patient should do now?
   a ☐ Avoid using the bike until next week.
   b ☐ Avoid using the bike for several weeks.
   c ☐ Do the race, but very slowly.

5 What will the patient need to do if he needs injections for his holiday?
   a ☐ Return to the doctor.
   b ☐ Get the injections from someone at reception.
   c ☐ Get the injections from a nurse.

c Write a conversation between two friends who are discussing what they do when they get ill. Use these questions to help you:

• What kinds of common illnesses do they get?
• What kind of medicine do they take?
• What other things do they do to try to feel better?
• Have they ever tried a 'cure' that didn't work?

◉ Review and extension

1 GRAMMAR

Tick (✓) the correct sentences. Correct the wrong sentences.

1 ☐ It was the captain of the ship which was responsible.
   It was the captain of the ship who was responsible.
2 ☐ Throw away the tables whose legs are broken.
3 ☐ The film review, that came out yesterday, wasn't positive.
4 ☐ I moved into the room where you used to live in.
5 ☐ Then Rachel said me that she wanted to leave.
6 ☐ It's a lovely day, so I suggest having a picnic by the river.

2 VOCABULARY

Tick (✓) the correct sentences. Correct the wrong sentences.

1 ☐ Doctors are trying to develope new methods of treating patients without surgery.
   Doctors are trying to develop new methods of treating patients without surgery.
2 ☐ Marcus can't race or train for three months and he isn't treating this very well.
3 ☐ The cost of medicine is a problem in the develop world.
4 ☐ You should take care for yourself now you're pregnant.
5 ☐ I feel weak. I'm sure I'm coming down with something.
6 ☐ Give her something before she loses consciousness!

3 WORDPOWER *come*

Complete the sentences.

1 The bill at the restaurant came __to__ over €200!
2 I came _____ an old photo of you while I was cleaning out the cupboard.
3 Grandma's dream has finally come _____ . We bought her the chance to drive a Formula 1 car for the day.
4 We had to throw the whole dinner in the bin. I've come to the _____ that I am not a master chef.
5 The name Elvis has come _____ a lot today. Every visitor to the museum has asked about him.
6 We're just going to advertise our business on the Internet unless we can come up _____ a better idea.

↻ REVIEW YOUR PROGRESS

Look again at Review Your Progress on p. 114 of the Student's Book. How well can you do these things now?
3 = very well   2 = well   1 = not so well

I CAN ...	
discuss new inventions	☐
discuss people's lives and achievements	☐
express uncertainty	☐
write an essay expressing a point of view.	☐

10A | IT MIGHT NOT HAVE BEEN HIS REAL NAME

1 GRAMMAR Past modals of deduction

a <u>Underline</u> the correct words to complete the sentences.

1 John's shoes are too small for the new school year. He <u>must</u> / *might* / *could* have grown a lot over the holidays.

2 We *must* / *may* / *could* have moved to Australia, but we decided to stay in England in the end.

3 That *can't* / *may* / *must* have been Sheila in the car, but I'm not too sure from this distance.

4 You *can't* / *may not* / *mustn't* have eaten all the cake. You'd be sick now!

5 The keys could be anywhere. I *can't* / *might* / *must* even have left them at the gym.

6 Wait, don't phone her yet. She *might* / *must* / *might not* have woken up.

7 Poor Andrés didn't eat for 24 hours. He *could* / *may* / *must* have felt really hungry.

8 I sent him a text, but he *can't* / *may not* / *mustn't* have received it because the reception isn't very good here. I'll try again.

9 Don't be silly, there was an instructor with them. What *can't* / *could* / *must* have gone wrong?

10 Sophie was in bed with the flu, so she *can't* / *may not* / *mustn't* have gone to the party.

b <u>Underline</u> the correct words to complete the text.

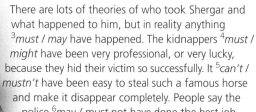

Shergar was a very successful champion race horse, in fact he [1]*can't* / *might* have been the best ever. His racing career ended in 1981, and he [2]*could* / *must* have made a lot more money for his owners from his celebrity status if he hadn't been stolen. This happened in 1983 and Shergar was never seen again.

There are lots of theories of who took Shergar and what happened to him, but in reality anything [3]*must* / *may* have happened. The kidnappers [4]*must* / *might* have been very professional, or very lucky, because they hid their victim so successfully. It [5]*can't* / *mustn't* have been easy to steal such a famous horse and make it disappear completely. People say the police [6]*may* / *must* not have done the best job of finding the horse because they [7]*could* / *must* have acted a lot more quickly – the truth is, they didn't have much evidence and the horse and its kidnappers were never found.

Some people say the kidnappers [8]*can't* / *must* have killed Shergar when the owners didn't agree to pay the kidnappers. This [9]*must* / *could* have been a tragedy for the owners and fans of Shergar. However, there [10]*must* / *may* have been a happier ending. Of course, Shergar can't be alive today because this happened so many years ago. Being optimistic, he [11]*can't* / *might not* have been killed by the kidnappers. He [12]*must* / *could* have died a natural death somewhere safe. We will probably never know.

c ▶ 10.01 Listen and check.

2 VOCABULARY Adjectives with prefixes

a Complete the sentences by adding a negative prefix to the adjective in brackets.

1 I am writing this letter of complaint because I was completely <u>dissatisfied</u> (satisfied) with the hotel facilities.

2 The product sells very well, so it's _____ (logical) to stop making it.

3 The fact that the suspect has a lot of tattoos is completely _____ (relevant).

4 Mike, this is an _____ (expected) surprise. I haven't seen you for ages!

5 The view from the balcony is _____ (believable). You have to see it for yourself.

6 The laws of physics show that it is _____ (possible) to go back in time.

b Complete the text with negative forms of the adjectives in the box.

credible   experienced   formal   honest   patient
polite   probable   reasonable   regular   responsible
~~satisfied~~   successful

Sally had worked as a trainee chef in a hotel for six months, but she was already [1] <u>dissatisfied</u> with her job, especially the [2]_____ hours and [3]_____ customers. Also, Sally was still quite [4]_____, but the head chef used to get [5]_____ with her because she couldn't do everything. Sally started to lose her self-confidence. Maybe she had [6]_____ expectations? Was she just another [7]_____ trainee, and would it be [8]_____ to continue in a job which she couldn't do? It was highly [9]_____ that things would get better. Sally got some [10]_____ advice from her old teacher at college, who told her to leave. For some reason – perhaps it meant she was [11]_____, too – Sally didn't listen to this advice, and she stayed at the hotel. This might seem [12]_____, but five years later, Sally is now head chef. She always smiles when her trainees tell her they want to leave.

c ▶ 10.02 Listen and check.

3 PRONUNCIATION Word stress

a <u>Underline</u> the stressed syllables in the words in **bold**.

1 The new parts are quite **inexpensive**.

2 I find it **improbable** that they just happened to be in the same place at the same time.

3 The weather at this time of the year is quite **unpredictable**.

4 I won't go on a trip as **disorganised** as this one again.

5 I've dropped it on the floor a few times, but it's **unbreakable**.

6 I can do it, but it's rather **inconvenient**, and I'm not very keen.

b ▶ 10.03 Listen and check.

1 GRAMMAR Wishes and regrets

a Underline the correct words to complete the sentences.

1 I wish I *would* / *could* / *did* speak another foreign language.
2 Do you ever wish you *had* / *have* / *would have* a brother instead of a sister?
3 I *wish* / *wished* / *hope* Sarah and Miguel get back together.
4 If only I hadn't *make* / *made* / *have made* so many mistakes in the first part of the test.
5 I wish you *would* / *should* / *might* think about somebody apart from yourself.
6 I'm sure all football managers wish they *were* / *are* / *would be* still able to play themselves.
7 You *would* / *should* / *will* have thought about that before you started shouting at everyone.
8 If you had three wishes, what *would* / *did* / *should* you wish for?
9 She wishes she *has* / *had* / *would have* spoken to the doctor a lot earlier.
10 Lana is nice, but I wish she *does* / *has done* / *did* more to help around the house.

b Complete the sentences. Use contractions where possible.

1 It's too bad you're not with us.
   I wish _____ **you were** _____ with us.
2 Jane, please listen to me for a moment.
   I wish you _____ for a moment, Jane.
3 I want to be ten years younger.
   She wishes that _____ ten years younger.
4 Mike doesn't live very close to the centre.
   Mike wishes _____ closer to the centre.
5 Why didn't I buy that dress?
   I wish _____ that dress.
6 It would be great if my horse wins the race.
   I _____ my horse wins the race.
7 It was wrong of me to be so rude to the shop assistant.
   I wish _____ so rude to the shop assistant.
8 It makes me so embarrassed when he lies.
   I wish _____ – it makes me so embarrassed.
9 I didn't study very hard in school, unfortunately.
   If only _____ harder in school!
10 My husband and I are watching a really boring film.
    I wish _____ this boring film.
11 Why didn't we go on this trip last year?
    We _____ on this trip last year.
12 It was a mistake to tell Eva.
    You _____ Eva.

2 VOCABULARY Verbs of effort

a Underline the correct words to complete the text. Then listen and check.

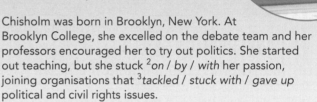

Fighting Shirley

Shirley Chisholm (1924–2005) was the first African American woman elected to the US Congress. In 1972, she became the first African American, and the first woman, to [1]*work on* / *pursue* / *overcome* the Democratic presidential nomination.

Chisholm was born in Brooklyn, New York. At Brooklyn College, she excelled on the debate team and her professors encouraged her to try out politics. She started out teaching, but she stuck [2]*on* / *by* / *with* her passion, joining organisations that [3]*tackled* / *stuck with* / *gave up* political and civil rights issues.

In 1968, she won a seat in the US Congress. There, 'Fighting Shirley' tirelessly worked [4]*with* / *by* / *on* civil rights issues. In 1972, she ran for president. She had to [5]*overcome* / *try out* / *pursue* plenty of racial discrimination; in fact, she was blocked from participating in the presidential debates, but she didn't give [6]*out* / *up* / *away* – she took legal action and was allowed to give one televised speech. Although she lost the nomination, she continued in Congress until 1983. She coped [7]*by* / *with* / *in* racism and sexism throughout her career, but 'Fighting Shirley' will always be remembered as a woman who fought for change.

b ▶ 10.04 Listen and check.

c Complete the sentences and questions with the words in the box.

cope with give up pursue overcome
stick with ~~tackle~~ work on

1 I think Olivia managed to ____ **tackle** ____ the task very well in the end.
2 It might seem difficult now, but it's important not to _____.
3 Is Chris really going to _____ this idea of running a marathon?
4 At first I couldn't _____ the pressure of working such long hours.
5 Few people realise how many difficulties he has had to _____ to get this far.
6 I need to _____ my pronunciation if my English is going to improve.
7 Don't complain – just _____ it!

10C EVERYDAY ENGLISH
Two things to celebrate today

1 USEFUL LANGUAGE
Describing how you felt

a <u>Underline</u> the correct words to complete the sentences.

1 When they took my winning ticket out of the bag, I was so *surprised* / *disappointed* / *interested*.

2 I *shouldn't* / *couldn't* / *wouldn't* believe it. It didn't seem real.

3 Trevor was *waiting* / *expecting* / *realising* the news, but it still came as a shock.

4 I was really *pleasant* / *pleasing* / *pleased*. I think I deserved to win first prize.

5 It was quite *a blow* / *news* / *expected*. I just stood there in shock.

6 The party was a disaster. I still can't *be* / *go* / *get* over it.

2 CONVERSATION SKILLS
Interrupting and announcing news

a Put the conversation in the correct order.

☐ **B** That's true, I guess. Well, thanks for telling me. I'd better get back.

☐ **B** What? I don't know about that. I'll have to think it over.

☐ **B** No problem, Luke. What's happened?

☐ **B** Hold on. I was just speaking to Tim yesterday. He didn't say anything.

☐ **A** Well, it's true. One more thing. Tim's gone to Masons.

☐1️⃣ **A** Hi, Lesley. Thanks for coming to see me.

☐ **B** Hang on a minute. Masons are our competitor. That's a disaster!

☐ **A** I know you won't believe this, but Tim has resigned.

☐ **A** Just a minute. There's something else we have to discuss. Would you be interested in taking Tim's job?

☐ **A** It's no tragedy. We haven't got any secrets he can tell them.

b ▶ 10.05 Listen and check.

3 PRONUNCIATION Consonant clusters

a ▶ 10.06 Listen and <u>underline</u> the words that have a consonant cluster (two or more consonant sounds together).

> In the <u>winter</u> of eighteen fifty-five, the people of Devon in England woke up to find the footprints of a strange animal in the snow.
>
> Some frightened people followed them, and the footprints went on and on ... for approximately a hundred miles – if their account is to be believed.
>
> The footprints went in a straight line through gardens and over walls and roofs.
>
> No one could explain the footprints, but since then many theories have been suggested.
>
> One of the strangest was that a kangaroo had escaped from a nearby zoo and jumped through the countryside!

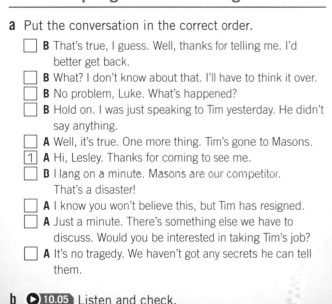

10D | SKILLS FOR WRITING
I forced myself to be calm

1 READING

a Read the beginning of a story. Put the events in the order they happened.

- [ ] She walks to the hotel.
- [ ] Jill finds evidence the hotel isn't closed.
- [ ] She asks for help.
- [ ] Jill switches on a light.
- [1] Tony gets married.
- [ ] Jill opens a letter.
- [ ] Tony invites Jill to visit him.
- [ ] She finds where the smell is coming from.
- [ ] Jill's car breaks down.

b Read the story again and tick (✓) the most appropriate answers.

1 How did Jill get to the hotel?
- a [ ] by car
- b [✓] on foot
- c [ ] It doesn't say.

2 What could Jill smell when she got there?
- a [ ] something difficult to recognise
- b [ ] something she instantly recognised
- c [ ] something unpleasant

3 How did Jill find the hotel?
- a [ ] by following directions
- b [ ] from memory
- c [ ] by chance

4 What happened to the car?
- a [ ] There was a technical problem.
- b [ ] There was an accident.
- c [ ] It ran out of petrol.

5 Why did Jill criticise Tony?
- a [ ] He had lied to her.
- b [ ] He refused to visit her.
- c [ ] He had insisted on the journey.

6 What did Jill feel guilty about?
- a [ ] having negative feelings about Tony
- b [ ] disturbing the hotel guests
- c [ ] turning on the light

7 What did Jill feel when she turned on the light?
- a [ ] relief
- b [ ] respect
- c [ ] regret

8 What stopped Jill from running out of the room?
- a [ ] She saw the message.
- b [ ] She smelled the food.
- c [ ] The door was locked.

The hotel was in darkness. Feeling tired from the walk, I stopped and looked around. What was going on? The place was obviously open – there were some cars and an unfamiliar smell from somewhere. It was strange finding a hotel – I couldn't remember seeing it on my map, but here it was.

If only my car hadn't broken down in the middle of nowhere, making me look for help. The journey hadn't been my idea. Tony had kept asking me to visit him and his new wife, and I had finally agreed. 'A few hours by car, Jill,' Tony had said.

I called out, 'Is anybody here? I need some help with my car.' Silence. Feeling guilty, I went inside. That strange smell was getting stronger, and I went towards it, almost falling down in the dark. Thankfully, I found a light switch and turned it on. I wish I hadn't.

I saw a table with a lot of food: meat, vegetables, fruit, cakes. All of it had gone bad and was rotten. Reaching for the door, I wanted to leave, but I noticed something else on that terrible table: a letter marked 'For Jill from Tony.' Inside, it said simply: 'You were too late for the party.' What could it mean?

2 WRITING SKILLS Making a story interesting

a Match 1–6 with a–f to make sentences.

1 [d] Walking away down the road,
2 [ ] Holding my head in my hands,
3 [ ] Shouting at the top of my voice,
4 [ ] Feeling weak and dizzy,
5 [ ] Not being in the best of moods,
6 [ ] Listening for a warning signal,

a I began to cry.
b I had to sit down for a moment.
c I hid behind a tree and waited.
d I resisted the temptation to look back.
e I sat in a corner and ignored everyone.
f I tried to get her attention.

b Complete the pairs of sentences with the gerunds and verbs in the box.

feeling / felt   ~~hearing / heard~~   hiding / hid   holding / held   realising / realised

1 a <u>Hearing</u> her voice shouting 'Come back,' I resisted the temptation to look back at her.
  b Lying on the ground and holding my breath, I <u>heard</u> someone walking close to me.

2 a _____ weak and dizzy, I had to sit down for a moment.
  b It _____ good to see Ben up and walking again after the accident.

3 a Darkness came and we soon _____ that we were completely lost.
  b Not _____ my mistake, I carried on as if nothing had happened.

4 a Listening for a signal, I _____ behind a tree, waiting anxiously.
  b He had a terrible day, _____ from the criminal who wanted to find him.

5 a The poor girl _____ her head in her hands, crying with frustration.
  b An old man came up, _____ a cup which he then offered to me.

3 WRITING

a Choose one of these first lines and continue the story. Write three paragraphs.

Looking into the terrible storm, I thought, 'How are we going to get out of this?'
I shook his hand and hurried away, hoping I'd never see him again.

UNIT 10
Reading and listening extension

1 READING

a Read the blog about regrets. Match the people 1–5 with the regrets a–e.

1 ☐ Jon (the author of the article)   a an experience at university
2 ☐ Amber   b an experience while looking for work
3 ☐ Shane   c not spending time with the family
4 ☐ Tony   d not studying enough in school
5 ☐ Sofia   e not travelling more

NEW POSTS | OLDER POSTS   SEARCH 🔍

ANY REGRETS? (Posted by Jon, 24 March)

A recent survey of over a thousand men and women in the UK aged over 25 found that if they could go back in time, 22% of married women would choose a different husband. Only 12% of men say they should have chosen a different wife! The survey also found that 30% of people wish they had chosen a different career, 35% wish they had chosen a different degree at university and 37% wish they had saved more money. Finally, 53% said they wish they had travelled around the world more when they were younger.

I'd have to get married before I could comment on the first two statistics. But if I could go back in time, would I choose a different university degree? Maybe. Would I have travelled more? Definitely, but then I think I really did all the travelling I could with the money I had. What about you? Would you have done anything different when you were younger? Do you have any big regrets?

AMBER
I do sometimes think back to one module at university. It was one of the last modules I had to do to finish my degree. I did OK in the module, but it was my last term and I just wasn't very motivated, so I didn't pay a lot of attention and afterwards, I threw away all my notes. I've recently changed jobs and my new job deals with many topics we covered in that module. I have often thought in the past few months – if only I had saved my notes and paid more attention in the lectures! But I guess it doesn't really matter. I'm learning new things every day at work and I don't think my life would've been that different if I had studied harder in that module and saved my notes. I suppose it would have been just a bit easier for my job now.

TONY
I wish I'd spent more time with my children when they were really young. I had a high-pressure job with long hours and regular trips overseas. So, although I tried to see my children as much as possible, I devoted a lot of my time to work because I thought I should be earning as much money as possible. On weekdays, I rarely saw them because I left for work before they woke up and got back after they'd gone to bed. Unfortunately, I think it's often easier to say 'no' to family than it is to work. Someone once told me: 'If you lose money, you can always earn more, but if you lose time, you can never get it back.' I didn't really understand what that meant at the time, but now I'm older, I do.

SHANE
Personally, I think the most important thing is to enjoy your life now and not think too much about the past and how things could have been different. I sometimes think about one job interview I went on just after finishing school. I'd planned to get the train to go to the interview, but because I prefer driving I decided to take the car and ended up getting lost in a city I didn't know very well. So I arrived late, which didn't create a good impression, and I wasn't offered the position. I was devastated at the time, but two months later, I got a much better job. So instead of regretting, I think we should look to the future and concentrate on overcoming problems we can actually change – I think everything happens for a reason.

SOFIA
I think that when you regret something, you can use that experience to work on your weaknesses and do better in the future. You learn from what went wrong and the mistakes you made, and make sure you do things differently next time. I was really irresponsible in school. I should have studied harder. But that was a good thing, because at university, I realised my mistake, and I really worked hard and appreciated the opportunity to study there. So in that case, regret really helped me change my behaviour.

b Read the blog again. Complete the sentences with the names in the box.

Jon   Amber   Sofia   Shane   Tony

1 _____ thinks regrets are not useful.
2 _____ regrets something that was probably unavoidable.
3 _____ regrets something for professional reasons.
4 _____ says you can learn from regrets.
5 _____ understands something better now than in the past.

c Read the blog again. Are the sentences true or false?

1 More men than women wish they had chosen a different partner.
2 Jon (the writer of the article) isn't married.
3 Amber didn't do well in the module because she didn't spend much time studying for it.
4 Shane thinks he didn't get the job because his train was late.
5 Tony generally only saw his children at weekends.
6 Sofia thinks her lack of effort in school made her a better university student.

d Write a paragraph about a regret that you or someone you know has. Remember to include:

- what the regret is
- why you or the person chose that course of action
- how your or the person's life would be different now if something had been different then.

2 LISTENING

a ▶ 10.07 Listen to five people talking about recent events. Match people 1–5 with situations a–e.

1 ☐ John	a a car accident
2 ☐ Martha	b a work meeting
3 ☐ Geno	c an interview for a university place
4 ☐ Barry	d losing an object
5 ☐ Emil	e meeting someone on the street

b Listen to the five people again. Match the emotions in the box with the people. There are three extra words you do not need.

angry   confident   exhausted   fortunate
not hopeful   regretful   surprised   worried

1 John _____   4 Barry _____
2 Martha _____   5 Emil _____
3 Geno _____

c Write a conversation between two people discussing an event neither of them are able to explain. Use these questions to help you:

- Where and when did the story take place?
- What happened?
- Why can't they explain what happened?
- Were they with any other people? Do they have an explanation for the event?

 # Review and extension

1 GRAMMAR

Tick (✓) the correct sentences. Correct the wrong sentences.

1 ☐ Thank you and I wish to hear from you soon.
   Thank you and I hope to hear from you soon.
2 ☐ We do hope you would enjoy the rest of your stay.
3 ☐ Sometimes I wish I were back at university again.
4 ☐ Goodbye, and I wish we can meet again soon.
5 ☐ Ryan wishes he spent more time there last summer.
6 ☐ Now I wish I hadn't let Chris join the team.

2 VOCABULARY

Tick (✓) the correct sentences. Correct the wrong sentences.

1 ☐ My friend Jane is a very responsable person.
   My friend Jane is a very responsible person.
2 ☐ The training facilities are satisfied for a club of this size.
3 ☐ Linda is really impatient, so don't keep her waiting too long.
4 ☐ I'm very unsatisfied with your response to my recent letter.
5 ☐ The police discovered her illegally use of company funds.
6 ☐ I can't cope with all these problems. I need some help.
7 ☐ I'd like to try snowboarding while we've got some snow.

3 WORDPOWER *way*

Underline the correct words to complete the exchanges.

1 A Do you want a lift to the station?
   B Don't worry, *there's no way / all the way /* <u>*we'll make our way*</u> after lunch.
2 A So Andy starts, then it's Rosie, then Amanda?
   B *One way or the other. / In some ways. / It's the other way round.*
3 A Would tomorrow about seven be all right?
   B *There's no way / One way or another / In some way* we can start that early.
4 A Is it difficult to get up the mountain?
   B No, there's a good path *the other way round / one way or another / all the way.*
5 A Are you sure you can get the car working again?
   B *All the way / One way or another / In some ways*, we will.

↻ REVIEW YOUR PROGRESS

Look again at Review Your Progress on p. 126 of the Student's Book. How well can you do these things now?
3 = very well   2 = well   1 = not so well

I CAN ...	
speculate about the past	☐
discuss life achievements	☐
describe how I felt	☐
write a narrative.	☐

VOX POP VIDEO

UNIT 1: Outstanding people

1a 📹 **What are your hobbies?**

a Watch video 1a. Match 1–6 with a–f to make sentences.

1 [b] Willemien likes   a watching sport.
2 ☐ Richard likes   b making music.
3 ☐ Hannah likes   c designing clothes.
4 ☐ Maddy likes   d playing music.
5 ☐ Heather likes   e drawing.
6 ☐ Maureen likes   f performing.

1b 📹 **Which hobby would you like to try?**

b Watch video 1b. <u>Underline</u> the correct words to complete the sentences.

1 Willemien *has never been* / <u>*used to go*</u> running.
2 Richard's hobby would involve *horses* / *travelling*.
3 Hannah wants to do *something with a friend* / *a water sport*.
4 Maddy would *not be* / *be* worried about how well she does this new hobby.
5 Maureen wants to try something that *is old-fashioned* / *people think is impossible*.
6 Heather thinks she will try painting after she *does the housework* / *has finished working*.

1c 📹 **How successful are you when you take up new activities?**

c Watch video 1c and tick (✓) the correct answers.

1 Willemien has a _____ % success rate.
   a ☐ 0
   b ☑ 50
   c ☐ 100

2 Richard only takes up activities which he _____.
   a ☐ wants to do
   b ☐ will be good at
   c ☐ needs to do

3 Hannah would probably be good at _____.
   a ☐ tennis
   b ☐ photography
   c ☐ dancing

4 When she tries something new, Maddy often _____.
   a ☐ needs help
   b ☐ fails
   c ☐ loses interest

5 Heather has no problem with _____.
   a ☐ motivation
   b ☐ time
   c ☐ work

Matt

Unit 2: Survival

2a 📹 **Which animal are you most scared of?**

a Watch video 2a. <u>Underline</u> the correct words to complete the sentences.

1 Lauren has a very *unusual* / <u>*common*</u> fear.
2 Matt is not so scared of cows *on their own* / *in groups*.
3 Anna is afraid of animals which *can harm her* / *are wild*.
4 Martina *could have died* / *didn't really need to worry*.

2b 📹 **What are some dangerous animals in a country you've visited?**

b Watch video 2b and tick (✓) the correct answers.

1 Lauren was in danger because _____.
   a ☑ of her shoes
   b ☐ she was alone
   c ☐ she was on a mountain

2 Matt was worried about snakes because he was staying _____.
   a ☐ in a hotel
   b ☐ in a tent
   c ☐ on a boat

3 Anna was surprised that the local people _____.
   a ☐ helped her
   b ☐ weren't afraid
   c ☐ had no special method

4 Martina was afraid of this animal because _____.
   a ☐ of a disease it spread
   b ☐ her friends were scared of it
   c ☐ she was living in a foreign country

5 What happened showed that Martina's fear was _____.
   a ☐ reasonable
   b ☐ silly
   c ☐ selfish

2c ■◀ **If you got too close to a lion, what would you do?**

c Watch video 2c. Match 1–5 with a–e to make sentences.

1 [e] Lauren
2 [ ] With a lion, Matt
3 [ ] With a shark, Matt
4 [ ] Anna
5 [ ] With a shark, Martina

a might attack the animal.
b wouldn't be able to scream.
c would lose consciousness.
d doesn't think climbing a tree would be effective.
e thinks it depends where it happened.

Unit 3: Talent

3a ■◀ **Can you tell me about a popular sport and why people like it?**

a Watch video 3a and tick (✓) the correct answers.

1 Eugenia talks about _____ marathons.
a [ ] running
b [ ] winning
c [✓] watching

2 Eugenia thinks the best thing about marathons is that _____.
a [ ] the pace is fast
b [ ] they are open to everyone
c [ ] you can run on the roads

3 James thinks that rugby is _____ football.
a [ ] more complicated than
b [ ] difficult to compare to
c [ ] basically the same as

4 Guy thinks Formula 1 is _____.
a [ ] dangerous
b [ ] the most popular sport
c [ ] full of surprises

5 Guy likes the fact that Formula 1 _____.
a [ ] races last two days
b [ ] goes over a longer period
c [ ] drivers need good qualifications

3b ■◀ **Are there any sports or activities you've been doing for a long time?**

b Watch video 3b. Underline the correct words to complete the sentences.

1 Eugenia was *good* / *bad* / *average* at sport at school.
2 Eugenia didn't *finish the marathon* / *run the marathon quickly*.
3 James *does athletics* / *plays football* at university.
4 Guy thinks that *talent* / *dedication* is more important for success in sport.

3c ■◀ **What do you think makes a successful athlete or sportsperson?**

c Watch video 3c and tick (✓) the correct answers.

1 Eugenia thinks the most important thing is to _____.
a [ ] have natural talent
b [ ] do a range of sports
c [✓] start young

2 When Eugenia was a girl, she wasn't very interested in _____.
a [ ] music
b [ ] sport
c [ ] anything

3 James thinks success in sport is to do with _____.
a [ ] how you think
b [ ] how fit and strong you are
c [ ] how you think and how strong you are

4 Guy thinks there are _____ factors involved.
a [ ] lots of
b [ ] not many
c [ ] one or two

5 Guy is the only person to talk about _____.
a [ ] training
b [ ] diet
c [ ] what sports people think about

Unit 4: Life lessons

4a ■◀ **How would you spend the money if you suddenly had £1,000,000?**

a Watch video 4a. Match 1–4 with a–d to make sentences.

1 [a] Ollie
2 [ ] Chris
3 [ ] John
4 [ ] Margaret

a names three things to spend money on.
b talks about a business opportunity.
c would spend the money on other people first.
d hasn't thought much about this before.

4b ■◀ **How would having a lot of money change your life?**

b Watch video 4b and tick (✓) the correct answers.

1 Ollie would feel _____.
a [✓] more secure
b [ ] lazier
c [ ] less motivated

2 Chris would _____.
a [ ] give up work
b [ ] not work as hard
c [ ] have more breaks

3 John thinks _____ would change.
a [ ] everything
b [ ] nothing
c [ ] few things

4 Margaret likes _____.
   a ☐ saving up to buy something nice
   b ☐ spending a lot of money
   c ☐ the responsibility of having a lot of money

5 The only person to see a negative side to this question is
   _____.
   a ☐ Ollie
   b ☐ John
   c ☐ Margaret

4c 🎥 Do you think winning a lot of money would have a positive or a negative effect?

c Watch video 4c. <u>Underline</u> the correct words to complete the sentences.

1 Ollie concentrates on the *positive* / *negative* consequences.
2 Ollie would choose a job which was *well paid* / *enjoyable*.
3 At the moment, Chris feels *satisfied* / *dissatisfied*.
4 At first, John would feel he didn't *want* / *deserve* the money.
5 Margaret would *give the money away* / *make it a positive experience*.

Unit 5: Chance

5a 🎥 Would you rather live somewhere really hot or really cold?

a Watch video 5a and tick (✓) the correct answers.

1 Anna _____ of wearing jumpers.
   a ✓ doesn't like the idea
   b ☐ understands the benefits
   c ☐ doesn't see the point

2 Anna and Matt both _____ about clothes.
   a ☐ agree
   b ☐ talk
   c ☐ complain

3 Matt feels _____ in hot conditions.
   a ☐ relaxed
   b ☐ ill
   c ☐ uncomfortable

4 Maibritt would prefer somewhere _____.
   a ☐ cold
   b ☐ neither cold nor hot
   c ☐ hot

5 Martina mentions California as an example of a place where _____.
   a ☐ it gets too hot
   b ☐ the weather doesn't change much
   c ☐ the weather makes her uncomfortable

5b 🎥 Have you ever experienced extreme weather?

b Watch video 5b. Match 1–4 with a–d to make sentences.

1 [c] Anna has experienced
2 ☐ Matt has experienced
3 ☐ Maibritt has experienced
4 ☐ Martina has experienced

a being unprepared for extreme weather.
b travelling from a hot place to a cold one.
c nothing extraordinary.
d a feeling of helplessness.

5c 🎥 What do you know about Antarctica?

c Watch video 5c. <u>Underline</u> the correct words to complete the sentences.

1 Anna wouldn't live in Antarctica because there *aren't many people* / *are too many dangerous animals*.
2 Matt had *higher* / *lower* expectations of Antarctica before he spoke to someone who worked there.
3 Unlike Anna and Matt, Maibritt mentions *animal life* / *industry* / *the weather* in Antarctica.
4 Maibritt would live there for a few *weeks* / *months*.
5 What Martina knows about Antarctica comes from *the media* / *personal experience*.
6 Martina *can* / *can't* imagine being there.

Unit 6: Around the globe

6a 🎥 What kind of places do you like to go to on holiday?

a Watch video 6a. Match 1–5 with a–e to make sentences.

1 [e] All the speakers talk about
2 ☐ Two of the speakers mention
3 ☐ Lauren likes
4 ☐ Lauren doesn't like
5 ☐ Jo mentions

a Italy.
b walking trips.
c the people you see.
d the food.
e the beach.

6b 🎥 What's the best holiday you've ever had?

b Watch video 6b. <u>Underline</u> the correct words to complete the sentences.

1 Rachel went on this holiday *after her wedding* / *10 days ago*.
2 The Maldives *met Rachel's expectations* / *disappointed her*.
3 Jo had *never* / *always* thought about having a holiday like this.
4 Jo travelled mostly by *bus* / *plane*.
5 Lauren's journey took longer because of *the heat* / *a problem with the boat*.
6 This delay *spoiled* / *didn't spoil* Lauren's holiday.

6c ■◀ **How do you think tourism will change in the future?**

c Watch video 6c and tick (✓) the correct answers.

1 Rachel thinks more people will _____.
   a ☐ stay at home
   b ✓ travel around their own country
   c ☐ go abroad

2 One reason for this is _____.
   a ☐ environmental issues
   b ☐ plane travel is cheap
   c ☐ people have a lack of options

3 Lauren disagrees with Rachel about _____.
   a ☐ what people think about the environment
   b ☐ the standard of hotels
   c ☐ the costs involved

4 Lauren thinks that most people will have _____.
   a ☐ eco-holidays
   b ☐ the same kind of holidays as now
   c ☐ more cultural holidays

5 Jo uses space tourism as an example of a direction which is _____.
   a ☐ completely different
   b ☐ a waste of money
   c ☐ of no personal interest

Unit 7: City living

7a ■◀ **Do you get easily stressed?**

a Watch video 7a and tick (✓) the correct answers.

1 Deborah considers stress to be _____.
   a ✓ a challenge
   b ☐ something to be avoided
   c ☐ a personal problem

2 An example of stress Deborah gives is _____.
   a ☐ difficult children
   b ☐ not doing things on time
   c ☐ life-or-death situations

3 Tony _____ gets into stressful situations.
   a ☐ never
   b ☐ occasionally
   c ☐ often

4 Tony's stressful situations are usually the result of _____.
   a ☐ where he lives
   b ☐ inconvenient phone calls
   c ☐ the demands of relatives

5 One way for Arian to relax is _____.
   a ☐ playing the piano
   b ☐ meeting friends
   c ☐ sport

6 Margaret thinks she is lucky because she _____.
   a ☐ has always been quite relaxed
   b ☐ is fit and healthy
   c ☐ has no stress in her life

7 Andrew gets stressed _____.
   a ☐ all the time
   b ☐ when he's driving
   c ☐ unless he listens to music

7b ■◀ **Do you think people are more stressed nowadays than they were fifty years ago?**

b Watch video 7b. Underline the correct words to complete the sentences.

1 Deborah bases her opinion on what *she has read* / *relatives have told her about the past*.

2 Arian *agrees* / *disagrees* with Deborah.

3 Margaret thinks it is particularly difficult for *younger* / *unemployed* people.

4 Margaret also thinks that *low salaries* / *long working hours* are an issue.

5 Margaret and Andrew both mention *the pace of life* / *difficult decisions to be made*.

6 Andrew talks about the *positive* / *negative* role of technology.

7c ■◀ **What do you like about the area where you live?**

c Watch video 7c. Match 1–6 with a–f to make sentences.

1 ☐d☐ Deborah likes
2 ☐ Tony criticises
3 ☐ Arian appreciates
4 ☐ Arian doesn't like
5 ☐ Andrew likes
6 ☐ Andrew dislikes

a socialising with the same group.
b the number of places to sit.
c the local transport.
d the cultural life.
e being near the sea.
f the standard of education.

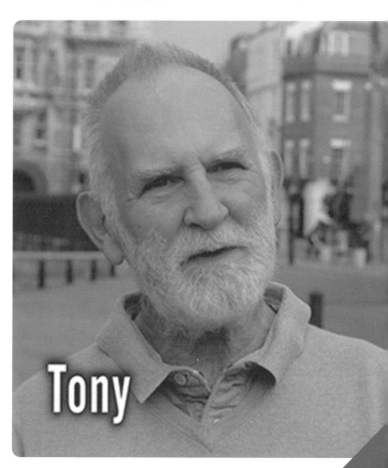

Tony

Unit 8: Dilemmas

8a ▶ Is it important to plan how you spend your money?

a Watch video 8a. Match 1–5 with a–e to make sentences.

1 [c] Caroline talks about
2 [ ] Dave and Caroline both mention
3 [ ] Jessie talks about
4 [ ] Colin and Gary agree that
5 [ ] Only Gary mentions

a planning is very important.
b being spontaneous with money.
c being happy with the money you have.
d buying property.
e wasting money.

8b ▶ Do you prefer using cash or cards?

b Watch video 8b. Underline the correct words to complete the sentences.

1 Caroline has a *slight* / *strong* preference for cash.
2 Dave prefers cash because this is *more traditional* / *easier*.
3 Jessie uses *cash machines* / *her phone* a lot in dealing with money.
4 Colin thinks cards are *more economical* / *easier to use*.
5 Gary's story about the café shows he doesn't *organise his cash very well* / *like cash very much*.

Jessie

8c ▶ Do you think people spend more money if they use a credit card than if they use cash?

c Watch video 8c and tick (✓) the correct answers.

1 Caroline thinks spending cash _____.
   a [ ] is just more interesting
   b [ ] makes you feel better about what you buy
   c [✓] has a more immediate effect on people
2 Dave speaks for _____ people.
   a [ ] the majority of
   b [ ] some
   c [ ] a significant amount of
3 Colin thinks _____ money affects people's spending habits.
   a [ ] the size of
   b [ ] greed of
   c [ ] seeing your
4 Gary _____ between cards and cash.
   a [ ] sees no difference
   b [ ] finds it difficult to choose
   c [ ] sees a big difference

Unit 9: Discoveries

9a ▶ What advice would you give me if I had a bad cold?

a Watch video 9a. Match 1–4 with a–d to make sentences.

1 [d] Lynne recommends
2 [ ] Steph recommends
3 [ ] Alwyn recommends
4 [ ] Chloe recommends

a not spreading infection.
b two kinds of drinks.
c not doing anything too demanding.
d covering yourself in something warm.

9b ▶ What do you think has been the biggest breakthrough in medical science?

b Watch video 9b. Underline the correct words to complete the sentences.

1 Lynne and Steph name *technology* / *medicine*.
2 Alwyn names a result of *research* / *medicine*.
3 Claire talks about health problems which *are the result of accidents* / *exist from birth*.
4 Claire believes the new treatment *is completely successful* / *has almost solved the problem*.
5 Chloe names DNA sequencing because it *has led to* / *was the result of* other breakthroughs.

9c ◼️◀ What medical invention would you most like to exist?

C Watch video 9c and tick (✓) the correct answers.

1 Lynne names a method of _____ the brain's
  information.
  a ☐ sharing
  b ✓ keeping
  c ☐ hiding

2 Steph names a treatment which would be _____.
  a ☐ universal
  b ☐ well known
  c ☐ fast-working

3 Alwyn thinks the invention will be based on _____.
  a ☐ a lucky guess
  b ☐ professional experience
  c ☐ previous research

4 Claire thinks the problem is that _____.
  a ☐ cancer can't be cured
  b ☐ there are many types of cancer
  c ☐ inventions take a long time

5 The tone of Chloe's answer is _____.
  a ☐ joking
  b ☐ disappointed
  c ☐ bitter

Unit 10: Possibilities

10a ◼️◀ What would be your dream job?

a Watch video 10a and tick (✓) the correct answers.

1 Alyssia bases her choice on _____.
  a ☐ financial rewards
  b ✓ her current position
  c ☐ the opportunity to be famous

2 In the army, Dan _____.
  a ☐ designs weapons
  b ☐ makes bombs safe
  c ☐ fixes vehicles

3 Dan wants to stay in the army _____.
  a ☐ for a long time
  b ☐ until he retires
  c ☐ for a short period

4 Lottie talks about a job which _____.
  a ☐ has no name
  b ☐ has long working days
  c ☐ involves organising events

5 Tim works with _____.
  a ☐ a range of ages
  b ☐ teenagers only
  c ☐ teenagers and young adults

6 Elizabeth says her priority is _____.
  a ☐ developing a successful business
  b ☐ her free time
  c ☐ doing something practical

7 Tom is _____ about his future career.
  a ☐ certain
  b ☐ undecided
  c ☐ confused

Alyssia

10b ◼️◀ What did you dream of becoming when you were a child?

b Watch video 10b. Match 1–6 with a–f to make
sentences.

1 ☐e Alyssia
2 ☐ Dan
3 ☐ Alyssia and Lottie both
4 ☐ Tim
5 ☐ Elizabeth
6 ☐ Tom

a gave up on an idea because of the lifestyle.
b realises it is probably too late to do this.
c wanted to design buildings.
d had no idea at all of a future profession.
e wanted to find objects from the past.
f had lots of different ideas.

10c ◼️◀ Is it ever too late to make a big change in your life?

c Watch video 10c. Underline the correct words to
complete the sentences.

1 Alyssia's grandfather started *learning languages* / *a new
  job* in a foreign country.
2 Dan *disagrees* / *agrees* with Alyssia.
3 Lottie thinks that change is possible in relationships if
  people *like each other enough* / *want the same thing*.
4 Tim *wants to think* / *definitely believes* that it is possible to
  make a change.
5 Elizabeth thinks that it is a question of *motivation* / *chance*.
6 Tom thinks that age is *important* / *unimportant*.

AUDIOSCRIPTS

Unit 1

▶ **01.01**

The other day I was walking down the street when I saw Sam Carter, you know, the famous film director. I was really excited because he has been one of my favourite directors for ages and I watch his films all the time. 'What is he doing here?' I thought to myself. There was only one way to find out. Sam was going into a café, but I stopped him before he got inside and said, 'Hi, Sam!' He smiled at me and we started to talk outside. Me and Sam Carter! He always looks so serious in photos, but he's a really friendly guy. In the end, Sam invited me for a coffee. Then he told me why he was in town. His film company were making a new film and they have lots of new faces in it, just ordinary people, but they need some more. 'How about you?' Sam asked. 'Have you watched any of my films? Do you want to be in one?' I was so shocked I dropped my cup on the floor! The hot coffee went all over Sam; he screamed and ran outside. I lost my big chance!

▶ **01.02**

/e/: desert, helpful, identity, sensitive, slept
/ɪ/: desire, prizes, revise
/ɜː/: concerned, dessert, prefer, service

▶ **01.03**

FABIO   Hi, there. Have you got five minutes?
GABRIELLA   Sure. What did you want to talk to me about?
F   Well, I'm doing a triathlon next month. Didn't you read my post?
G   No, I haven't seen it. A triathlon, wow! What for? It sounds really tough!
F   It's not easy, yeah, swimming, cycling, then running.
G   Which of those is the most difficult?
F   All of them! Er, weren't you a good swimmer once?
G   Yeah, once. What are you looking at me like that for?
F   Do you think you could coach me?
G   I don't know whether I've got enough time. Can I think about it and phone you later?
F   No problem. That's great! I'll swim a lot faster with your help.
G   Who knows? You might win!

▶ **01.04**

You don't need to get a very expensive camera. These have a lot of functions you just don't need. Do you understand what I mean?
But whatever camera you buy, read the instructions carefully. Make sure you know what your camera can do. Have you got that?
When you take a photo, the most important thing is the light. Basically, the more light, the better, so choose the right time of the day and place. Do you get the idea?
Always remember to keep still. If the camera moves about, you get a bad photo.
Another thing to remember is to take your time. Only real professionals can take good photos in a hurry. Is that clear? Do you want me to explain any of this again?

▶ **01.05**

1   I must go and see her soon.
2   The nurse said I must eat less bread.
3   We've got to have more help.
4   Sorry, you can't take one with you.
5   Haven't any of the people arrived?
6   Sarah said she didn't do the homework.
7   Claudia has been there, hasn't she?
8   The shop might open again.
9   We can't use our phones here.
10   Children mustn't play ball games.

▶ **01.06**

MICHAEL   What are you reading?
SARAH   An article about this guy … Frane … Selak.
M   Who's that?
S   He's a man from Croatia … They've called him the unluckiest man in the world. It looks like he's had an incredible life.
M   Incredible, how?
S   Well … It started in the 1960s. He says he was on a train that came off the tracks and crashed into a river – 17 people died, but he survived!
M   Lucky.
S   He did break his arm, though. Anyway, the next year he was flying on a small plane, which also crashed. The incredible thing was that as it was about to crash, one of the doors opened – the article says it had a fault – and he was sucked out. He landed safely but nobody on the plane survived!
M   That's amazing!
S   I know. Then a few years later, he was in a bus accident. There was heavy rain and the bus driver lost control on the wet roads and crashed into a river. He survived, although four people drowned. Then he was in a car that caught fire while he was driving it on the motorway. He managed to get out with seconds to spare before the fuel tank exploded.
M   Wow. I don't think I ever want to travel with this guy …
S   Yeah, but that's not all … He got hit by a bus in 1995.
M   But he was OK?
S   Of course. And then the year after, he had another car crash. He was driving on a road in the mountains and he had to turn out of the way of a lorry coming in the other direction. So then his car went off the edge of the mountain and when it hit the bottom, it exploded. But Selak was OK because he'd managed to jump out just before it went over the edge. He was found holding onto a tree near the side of the road.
M   That's just amazing.
S   Yeah.
M   But I don't know whether he's unlucky or extremely lucky.
S   Well, the story's not finished yet. Apparently in 2003, he won the Croatian lottery. With the first ticket he'd ever bought.
M   No way!
S   That's what it says! So in the end, he's definitely lucky, not unlucky!
M   Or maybe a mix of both.
S   Yeah, maybe.
M   Do you think it's true, all that? Can all these things really happen to one person?
S   I don't know. I don't think everyone believes it. And it says there's no record of any plane crash in Croatia in the 1960s.
M   Mmm.
S   So I don't know. What do you think?
M   Well, it's a fascinating story, so I want to believe it's true. But who knows?
S   Yeah.
M   What did he do with the lottery money, by the way?
S   Well, first he bought himself a luxury home, that kind of thing. But then he decided to sell it and give most of the money away to friends and family because he thought that money couldn't buy happiness.
M   Well, it could all be true then. Anyone who would give away all their lottery winnings must be a really good person, so they wouldn't make up a story like that. I think that's quite inspiring.

Unit 2

▶ **02.01**

One afternoon some years ago, I was thinking about what to do when my friend Janice phoned. She was in a good mood because she had finished all her exams. She came round and we decided to go for a walk in the mountains. We hadn't gone very far – only 4,000 steps on my phone app – when the weather suddenly changed. Until that moment, it had been warm and sunny, but the sky very quickly turned dark and it began to rain heavily. We hadn't taken our coats or umbrellas with us, and we were getting very wet. We ran to a nearby tree to take shelter, hoping the rain would soon stop, but ten minutes later the temperature dropped and it started snowing. We walked back the way we had come earlier, but the small bridge we had crossed before was now under water, as the river had burst its banks. I tried to phone for help, but my battery had died and Janice had forgotten to bring her phone. By then it was getting dark and we were very scared. Imagine our relief when suddenly we saw the lights of a farmer's truck. He was out looking for a lost sheep – and he rescued us!

▶ **02.02**

1   We'd been swimming in the sea.
2   The fishing had been fun and I wanted to try it again.
3   I'm not sure what's been decided.
4   What had they been doing on the journey?
5   He's been told to rest at home.
6   Tim had been learning to ride a bike.
7   She'd never been climbing in her life.
8   Her husband's been worrying about her.
9   The expedition had been my idea at first.
10   The TV people had been trying to interview him.

▶ **02.03**

MARIO   Hi, Silvia. Are you coming camping with us?
SILVIA   If you still want me to, sure.
M   Great. It should be good fun unless the weather gets bad.
S   As long as we get a couple of days of decent weather, I don't mind. What do I need to take?
M   The usual stuff. When I get home, I'll text you the list I've made just in case. You don't need to worry about food though. I've packed enough provided you like pasta. That's the easiest thing to make.
S   Fine. In case we run out of pasta, I'll take some tins and rice.
M   Good idea. If you want, bring some cards. We could play at night.
S   I'll do that provided I don't forget. Text me tomorrow as soon as you get up.
M   OK. Remember to buy pepper spray because we might see bears.
S   If I see a bear, I'll run all the way home!

▶ **02.04**

MIKE   It's a beautiful day!
LUCY   It's lovely, isn't it? Why don't we go to the beach?
M   Yes, let's do that, shall we?
L   We could drive but let's walk. We need the exercise.
M   We do, don't we? I'll get my things.
L   Last time you forgot your towel.
M   I didn't have it with me, did I, so I borrowed yours. Anyway, let's go.
…
L   That was great, wasn't it? I feel really hungry now.
M   Me too. This place looks good.
L   Yeah, we've been here before, haven't we? It does really good pizza.
M   That's right. Oh, I haven't got my wallet. You couldn't lend me some money, could you?

L First a towel, then your wallet. You never remember anything.

M Well, we're friends, aren't we? Let's go inside.

▶ **02.05**

1 **A** You're so good at singing.
　B Do you think so?
2 **A** Your hair is amazing!
　B I'm glad you like it.
3 **A** You really managed to get it just right.
　B Guess it's not bad.
4 **A** The colour is just perfect.
　B It's not bad, is it?
5 **A** It's so tasty!
　B It's all right.
6 **A** That was a lovely present!
　B I'm glad you like it.

▶ **02.06**

1 It was a great idea, wasn't it?
2 You don't know where Oxford Street is, do you?
3 That's obvious, isn't it?
4 They just didn't understand, did they?
5 He hasn't finished university yet, has he?
6 I'm not on the team, am I?
7 They will be able to do it, won't they?
8 You've been there before, haven't you?
9 She's forgotten all about it, hasn't she?
10 She's not going to agree, is she?

▶ **02.07**

ANNOUNCER A woman reported missing over two weeks ago has been found safe. Alicia Lone, who works as an assistant chef, was expected home shortly after 9 pm. Her family were not initially concerned, as she had recently got involved with a sports club and often went there after work before returning home. But when she still hadn't returned by early the next morning, they contacted the police. Here's Michael Sanderson with the full report.

REPORTER When Alicia Lone went missing 16 days ago, it seemed a complete mystery. Police knew she had left work by car after her shift finished at 8:15 pm, but after that, there were no signs of her at all. But yesterday, the mystery was solved – Lone was found alive inside her car, under over a metre of snow, where she had managed to survive for 15 days. Police say there was no problem with her car and that it seems she got into trouble when she decided, because of the heavy snow, to take a different route. But she didn't get very far – her car was found two kilometres from the main road. Police say she stopped soon after turning because the road was so bad, but was unable to turn back. She then spent a night in the car expecting to be able to get home the next day, but the snow got heavier and her car got totally stuck. Earlier, I spoke to Police Sergeant Granger, who gave us further details.

POLICE OFFICER We've only been able to speak very briefly to Lone at the hospital so we don't know the full story yet. But it seems she turned up that road to try and avoid some of the snow on the main road, but obviously she didn't get anywhere and became stuck. She couldn't get a signal to phone for help. Very few cars travel around this area during this winter period unless there's some special reason, so she wasn't able to get anyone's attention to ask for help either. So nobody saw her until yesterday, when a road maintenance crew went up there to check on the state of the road and saw the car under all the snow. When they found her, she was basically asleep. We could see she'd been eating in the car, that she had had some food in there, and she'd also been drinking melted snow. But it's incredible that she was able to survive with so little, really.

R Did they give you any idea at the hospital *how* she survived?

PO Well when she was found, her body temperature was very low and they think that because of the cold weather her body just kind of went to sleep, like some animals do in winter. She couldn't speak or walk when we found her. So the doctors say her body basically went to sleep, so she didn't need much food or water. But she was very lucky.

R And do they think she's going to be OK?

PO They think so, yes – she's going to make a full recovery. She has a few problems now but she should get over them fine.

R So, it's a story with a happy ending, fortunately. We'll give you more news on Lone's condition as soon as we get it.

Unit 3

▶ **03.01**

When I was at school, I didn't think I was good at anything. The other kids picked things up really quickly, but I didn't, and I thought that some kids looked down on me as some kind of loser. The only thing that interested me was cars, and I spent ages in the garage with my mum's old car looking into how it worked. My mum wasn't into cars at all, though, and she was tired of me going on about them all the time. Anyway, one day there was a school trip. I woke up early to catch the coach. We were going down the road when the coach suddenly stopped. I thought we had run out of petrol, but the driver told us there was an engine problem and he would have to call the garage. I went to see for myself and quickly figured out what to do: I just needed to put back a cable. After ten minutes, the coach was on the road again. After that, everyone looked up to me and I realised there was something I could do well. When I left school, I set up my own car repair business and now I'm doing really well.

▶ **03.02**

MARIANA Have you heard of this writer Daniel Kalder?
LIAM Yes, I read *Strange Telescopes* some time ago. It's a brilliant book.
M I agree. Kalder has got this ability to make a serious statement but make you laugh at the same time.
L It really is outstanding. I just wish I had some talent for writing.
M Kalder is successful because he's spent so many years improving his style. That kind of hard work is exceptional.
L True. I don't think many people have heard of Kalder yet, but he has the potential to be a really well-known writer.
M He is very skilled at what he does, so good luck to him.

▶ **03.03**

Shantelle Gaston-Hill has just broken a new world record! Yesterday in Manchester, England, she ran a half-marathon – that's just over 21 kilometres – in 2 hours, 16 minutes and 3 seconds. And she did it backwards! Shantelle is 32 years old and this is the second time she has beaten all the best runners in the world. From March 2017 to January 2019, Shantelle held the world record and now, just ten months later, she has set a new world record!
Shantelle started retro-running – running backwards – for fun, but soon after she began to take her hobby more seriously. But that's not all. She has also completed five marathons and eight ultra-marathons, too. It's safe to say that Shantelle has been running forwards and backwards for quite a while!
Every time she has raced, she has represented a charity. This time Shantelle represented YoungMinds, a mental health charity for children and young people. She wants to show people that consistent training and determination can get extraordinary results.

▶ **03.04**

Everyone thinks that professional sportspeople get paid a lot of money to compete, but this is not always true. The top athletes in smaller sports like handball, mountain running and women's cricket don't earn much money. Such sports are very competitive and the athletes train hard, but even if they represent their country, they often can't make a living from their sport. Unfortunately, victory in championships and new world records very often don't mean money, especially if the sport isn't popular on TV. But maybe this doesn't matter if the athletes enjoy what they do and spectators are happy to watch them perform and cheer for them. Money isn't everything, after all.

▶ **03.05**

ELENA I know you like athletics, but do you ever take part in competitions?
DIMA Sometimes – in fact I'm going to compete in the national championships next weekend.
E So you're almost a professional athlete then?
D Not really, it's hardly a profession but I do a lot of training and I'm hoping for a good performance. There'll be a lot of strong competitors and I'll have to perform really well on the day.
E So victory might be yours then, and we'll welcome the victorious champion home?
D Don't laugh, I might win!

▶ **03.06**

1	game	came	6	save	safe
2	beach	peach	7	pie	buy
3	ferry	very	8	pig	pick
4	simple	symbol	9	pack	back
5	girl	curl	10	have a	have to

▶ **03.07**

TINA Mark, I've been going through my cupboards and I've found some old photos from school. Do you want to look at them?
MARK Yeah, of course!
T Right, well, here they are. There are quite a lot ... Look at this one – do you remember her? Martina?
M Oh yes, Martina ... I do. She was brilliant at maths and all those kinds of subjects, wasn't she?
T Yeah. I wonder what happened to her. Probably became an economist or something.
M Yeah, I reckon. Anyway, I bet she's really successful, whatever she's doing.
T Oh, and here's one with you in it.
M Yeah, but who's that with me? I don't recognise her.
T That's Julia. Don't you remember her?
M Oh yeah, Julia, of course. She was really talented at sports, wasn't she?
T Yeah, tennis especially, I think.
M Well, I haven't seen her for years anyway.
T No. I know that she lives in Madrid now.
M Really?
T Yeah, she's been living there a while. I don't know what she's doing there though.
M I didn't like her much, to be honest. She was always a bit too ... competitive.
T Yeah, I know what you mean. She wasn't exactly my favourite person either. We both represented the school at athletics, but she wasn't very friendly. And she was always going on about tennis!
M I wouldn't say she was unfriendly, just too competitive for me!
T Hmm, look at this one. It's me, you and Mr Edwards.
M The best teacher ever!
T Hmm, I'm not sure about that.
M Come on! I thought he was exceptional. He was the only one that made me really feel I had any ability. You know what I was like at school. But he really seemed to believe in me.
T Well, I suppose I liked the fact that he made us try out new things. But anyway … have a look at this one.
M Oh, that's Sarah.
T Yeah. Didn't you fall out with her once? At a party or something?
M More than once, I think. We didn't get on – in fact, nobody at school got on with her.
T Right, let's move on quickly then! Here, look – it's our whole class, after a French lesson, isn't it?
M Yeah, look, there's the French teacher.
T Mrs Taylor.
M Yep. That classroom doesn't bring back too many happy memories, I have to say.
T But you have a talent for languages. You speak French really well now, and Spanish.
M Yeah, but the lessons at school weren't for me. I'd say that Mrs Taylor was skilled at teaching grammar, but we never did any kind of speaking practice, did we? I can only actually speak French because I've been to France so often and spoken to real French people.
T Mmm. Ah well, here's the last one. A school trip, but I don't know where we were.
M No, nor do I. That just looks like a field in the middle of nowhere! I used to love the school trips, though.

T Yeah, they were fun. And sometimes we even learned something!

M Sometimes, yeah. But most of the time it was just good to get out of school for a day!

Unit 4

▶ 04.01

Richard Morgan lives on a boat on a canal in London, but his life used to be very different. Richard left university in 2015 and got a great job at a law firm. It was interesting and well paid, but a very hard job. Richard used to work 12 to 14 hours a day and sometimes he would sleep at the office because it was so late. Richard realised that this kind of life was killing him. 'I was used to spending all my time at work. It was normal for me, that was the frightening thing,' Richard says.

On Sundays Richard would go for a walk down the canal and he always enjoyed this. So one day, when he had had enough, he decided to change his life completely. He gave up his job, bought a boat and said goodbye to his stressful life as a lawyer. 'It was a big contrast. I still haven't got used to the ducks waking me up, but it's a great life,' he says. 'My family and friends were shocked at first, but now they are used to visiting me on my boat and they know I'm happy.'

▶ 04.02

KATE So what's it like to be a firefighter, William?

WILLIAM It's really tough, much harder than I thought. The training is very rigorous and the instructors really stretch us.

K But you've finished all the training?

W Not yet. It's not so straightforward to become a firefighter. First, there's this arduous training schedule and then a tricky written test to do at the end.

K Well, you do like a challenge! It sounds like a very demanding job.

▶ 04.03

1	umbrella	6	attitude
2	pullover	7	result
3	useless	8	influential
4	sugar	9	enthusiasm
5	supper		

▶ 04.04

MARK Education is getting worse and worse in this country.

LILY Oh, I don't know. Some things are improving.

M Like what? Teachers don't know what they are doing.

L I'm not sure about that. They work very hard.

M Yes, but they need more training.

L Maybe you're right, but teachers are not the real problem.

M True – kids just don't want to study.

L Really, do you think so?

M I do. They spend far too much time playing on their phones.

L I know what you mean, but on the other hand, technology is so central.

M Hang on, someone's texting me …

▶ 04.05

1 **A** It was an absolutely terrible hotel! I never want to go there again.
   B Oh, I don't know. It wasn't that bad.
2 **A** I really didn't like that film. It was so boring!
   B Oh, I don't know. It wasn't that boring.
3 **A** I loved that restaurant. The menu was really original.
   B Oh, I don't know. It wasn't that original.
4 **A** Have you seen that new shop? It looks great!
   B Oh, I don't know. It doesn't look that great.
5 **A** I thought the meeting today was far too long.
   B Oh, I don't know. It wasn't that long.

▶ 04.06

REPORTER I'm here on the grounds of the University of South Norwood, on a day that many of the students here will remember for a long time – graduation day. I took the chance to speak to some of them today about this – you could maybe call it a life-changing day.
OK, so I'm here with Carl. How are you feeling today?

CARL Pretty happy! It's not been easy. I had to work really hard this summer, a lot of revision, a lot of time spent in the library or in my room with a pile of books in front of me. It was all pretty gruelling really.

R Was it worth it?

C Oh, yeah, definitely. I feel great today. All the hard work paid off, I suppose. It's really been a struggle at times – I'm a full-time student, or I was, but I also had to work in a restaurant for 20 hours a week to support my studies. So it was a challenge sometimes. But today, being here with my family and getting my diploma – it's great, and it's why I put all that effort in.

R Great, well, congratulations!

C Thank you.

R So, Samantha, are you happy today?

SAMANTHA Of course! It means I've finished university now and I can go and find a job!

R So how has it been? It must have been a lot of work for you to get through.

S Well, yeah, I suppose. It's been tricky sometimes, but it's never been a struggle. I found most parts of my course quite straightforward. I always did quite well in my exams, so it wasn't a big problem really. The only thing was that I had to do my last three exams in two days – that was quite demanding. But in the end, you just do it – you're forced to really, there's no choice.

R Enjoy your day.

S Thanks.

R OK, so we're going to speak to Luke. How are you feeling?

LUKE OK, I suppose. Yeah, pretty good.

R You're not happy that you're graduating today?

L Yeah, I am happy. But I'm a bit disappointed as well. I didn't get the grade I was hoping for, so today, well, I'm happy, but I'm also a little bit … sad, I suppose.

R Sorry to hear that. Do you want to tell us what went wrong?

L I don't know really. In my last two exams, I just didn't get very good marks, and that influenced my final grade for my whole degree. I had a really bad cold in the week before those last two exams, so I think that affected me a bit. But unless you're seriously ill on the day of the exam itself, the university doesn't take things like that into account. I don't think it's right because it probably had an effect on my performance in those two exams.

R Well, I hope you enjoy your day despite your disappointment.

L Thanks.

R So, Jane, how are you feeling right now?

JANE I feel great! And relieved! It means I can relax a bit.

R What kinds of things will you remember about your time at university?

J Mainly being tired, I think! It's been a pretty punishing time. As you can probably tell, I'm a bit older than most of the students graduating today. I was 40 when I decided to go to university. None of my friends had ever gone to university, nobody in my family. So that really stretched me, really challenged me. But that's also why I wanted to do it.

R And what's the future for you now? Have you found a job yet?

J Well, I already had a job – I never gave it up. But hopefully, having a degree will open up a few more opportunities for me at work. I was a bit stuck before, I think.

R Thanks, and best of luck.

J Thanks.

Unit 5

▶ 05.01

KATY Have you read this article, Josh? It says there's a good chance the next generation will live to be 150 years old!

JOSH Who knows? What it says may be true. But what evidence is there?

K Advances in medicine will certainly be a factor, and people won't die from all sorts of diseases common today. Also, technology will probably make everyday life easier.

J Fine, but I doubt if many people will want to live that long. It's unlikely that it'll be much fun to be 150.

K The article says that we will probably be able to work until that age. There's a good chance that machines will do all the hard work, like washing and cleaning, so that we can do different tasks, like critical thinking.

J Interesting. I'm sure there'll even be a special Olympics for people over 100!

K Yes, it's bound to happen, so start training!

▶ 05.02

1	think	7	the
2	athletic	8	breathing
3	breath	9	clothes
4	Earth	10	either
5	length	11	leather
6	month	12	though

▶ 05.03

Let's travel to the year 2059! We won't be living on Earth because pollution and wars will have destroyed the old planet. Instead, planet Zeus will be our home. Giant spaceships will have transported everyone and everything from Earth before it exploded in 2055. Zeus won't be a bad place to live, and some things will go on as normal. Adults will be going to work every morning. Children will be studying at school and old people will be complaining about almost everything. Many things will be different, though. Because of the different atmosphere, our hair will have turned green – at least it won't have fallen out – and we will be walking about in space suits. Special tablets will have replaced food and drink, so we won't be cooking at all, and we won't be eating out at restaurants. Yes, life will have changed quite a lot.
Welcome to 2059 and the future we will have created.

▶ 05.04

MAGDA You know, I'm seriously thinking of taking this job in Paris.

ROMAN No wonder! One good thing about it is the higher salary. It's basically a promotion.

M True, but the trouble with that is more pressure and stress. A big disadvantage of the position I've been offered is that I'll have too much to do.

R Come on, one of the best things about you is how you respond to a challenge.

M I suppose so … Another problem with this job offer is that I'll need to improve my French – and fast!

R No need to worry about that either. The advantage of living and working in a foreign country is that you learn the language quickly.

M You have an answer to everything!

R The only drawback of the job I can see is the size of the company. Do you really want to work in a company that big?

M If they pay me enough money, yes!

▶ 05.05

A How about eating out tonight for a change?

B It's an idea, I suppose. Where shall we go?

A There's a new Thai place which has just opened.

B Mm, I don't know about that. I'm not so keen on spicy food.

A Well, there's the Italian place just up the hill.

B That might be worth a try, and it's not far.

A Let's walk there. It's a lovely day.

B Yes, that makes sense. I need the exercise!

A We could invite Amelia and Rob, too.

B That's not a bad idea. They'd need to drive there, though.

A Then they could give us a lift if we feel too lazy to walk back.

B That's a possibility, although we might have to invite them in for a coffee or something.

A So I've got an excuse to make one of your favourite lemon cakes.

B That's a great idea! You haven't made one for ages.

▶ 05.06

1 The trouble is it could take a long time to get the money.
2 The good thing about it is we're not far away from the centre.
3 The problem is people are starting to talk about her.
4 The advantage is the price isn't very high.

5   The drawback is no one really knows what's going to happen.
6   The advantage is we can see a lot more of each other.
7   The trouble is I'm not sure I've got time to help him.
8   A definite disadvantage is it means selling the car.

▶ **05.07**

ANDREW   What's that you're reading, Fran?
FRAN   It's just a news story. It's about a supermarket chain. It has most of the products that a normal supermarket has, but it doesn't sell anything with packaging – so nothing's sealed in plastic, not fruit, not vegetables, not even meat or eggs.
A   Really? How does that work?
F   Well, you just take along your own bags, or boxes, or whatever.
A   Oh, I see … Isn't that a bit complicated?
F   Or you can actually get bags there. But then you bring them back and use them again and again.
A   Well, I suppose it sounds like a good idea. But I don't think I'll be going to a supermarket like that by choice.
F   Why?
A   Well, when I do the shopping I just want to get everything done quickly. I don't want to have to worry about bringing my own boxes or packing things myself.
F   But it's much more environmentally friendly!
A   Sure, I imagine it is, but I'm too busy for that kind of thing. And anyway, I already do quite a lot. I'm aware that we have to think about global warming, so I don't use the car too much, I throw litter in the bin, I turn the tap off when I'm brushing my teeth, that kind of thing.
F   I really don't think that taking some extra bags to the supermarket is going to take you that much time! Just think of all the damage that's caused by plastic packaging. Producing it pollutes the Earth's atmosphere and that's the kind of thing that causes climate change.
A   Well …
F   But it's not just that – it has a big impact in general. A lot of packaging ends up in the sea, in rivers …
A   I know. You're probably right. I suppose I'm probably just a bit lazy.
F   Well, I know it's not easy. But there are lots of things I think we could all do to reduce our carbon footprint …
A   Like what?
F   Well, only taking public transport, for example. Never using the car.
A   Not easy.
F   I know, but there's a difference between 'not easy' and 'impossible.' Or we could all become vegetarian.
A   Does that help the environment?
F   Yes, because producing meat actually uses a lot of energy and water, much more than producing vegetables.
A   Does it? Oh. I'd no idea.
F   And it takes up more space, too. More land, I mean, to farm all those big cows …
A   Well, I guess that could be a good reason to cut down on meat. But do you really think people are going to be happy to change their lifestyles like this?
F   No, that's my point. We could all do more, but we don't. We just talk about what we should do.
A   Personally, I think there's a chance that technology will save us. You know, if we're able to come up with technology that doesn't harm the environment, like electric cars, factories that don't pollute the air, really efficient machines that don't use much energy …
F   Yeah, there's always that hope, but I think we'll have destroyed the planet before we manage to come up with smart enough technology.
A   I suppose we'll see. I'm not as pessimistic as you, though.
F   Well, one thing's for sure – if we don't start to deal with the problem, then people on this planet will be paying for it for a long time.

Unit 6

▶ **06.01**

ELENA   Hi, Max, glad to see you. How's your summer?
MAX   Boring! I'm looking forward to going back to college. Sitting in front of the computer all day is not my idea of a holiday.
E   Why don't you go somewhere to have a break? I think it's really important to get away from everything once in a while.
M   Travelling is a waste of time. I remember visiting Paris last spring. I tried to see the *Mona Lisa* in the Louvre, but there were so many people I couldn't even get in the room, which was just as well as I'd forgotten to take my camera. Anyway, I'm not interested in walking around in crowds of tourists.
E   Sorry to hear that – but look, stop being so negative. You obviously like art, that's why you were in the Louvre, so why not do something connected with that? I can see you doing something creative.
M   I've tried painting and I wasn't too bad at it.
E   There you are, you may go on to be in the Louvre yourself!

▶ **06.02**

Welcome to Niagara Falls! This is your personal audio guidebook. Remember to turn the volume up quite high because it's pretty noisy here. You can hear the water pouring down the Falls, millions of litres every minute. If you want to admire the view, press the red button to stop the guide, and then the blue button to continue and go on listening. It's amazing to think that the Falls have been here for 10,000 years. Basically, ice melting into the Niagara river made it powerful enough to cut a huge piece out of the rock. More about this later. Back to today: millions of tourists come to visit the Falls each year. Having so many visitors is great, but all the activity causes a lot of damage, so we are trying to protect the Falls as much as possible. So …

▶ **06.03**

The Grovepark Hotel is located in a perfect setting on the outskirts of Casterbridge just half an hour away from the city centre and minutes from the hiking trails going up into the Wessex hills. It's an ideal conference venue with a number of features delegates will appreciate. Whether you're outside relaxing on the terrace admiring the views over your coffee, or inside in the lobby bar, you'll feel completely at home.

▶ **06.04**

a   We had some superb meals in an excellent local restaurant.
b   These ideas are a big contrast to what we heard yesterday.
c   The Pyramids in Egypt are the most impressive structures I've ever seen.
d   Their discussion lasted two hours.
e   We can't destroy the original document.
f   The train terminal is a short walk from the airport.

▶ **06.05**

Speak any language in 30 days! That's right, with our new online course, any language can be learnt effortlessly and perfectly. This is made possible by an amazing piece of software which today is being used by thousands of people studying 25 different languages in the comfort of their own homes. It's so simple. All the work is done online and the course is complete. No expensive extras have to be bought. But don't listen to us, listen to our customers: 'I was promoted back in January, but I needed to improve my English. This course had been recommended to me by a colleague, so I bought it and the results were amazing! Now I am being considered for an overseas post and I'm hoping my salary will be increased.'
'I have been given a completely new direction in life by this course. Now I can communicate with people all over the world. I'm so glad I was persuaded to sign up.'
What are you waiting for? Send us an email and you will be contacted by our customer care team in 24 hours. Goodbye! ¡Adios! Poka! Ciao!

▶ **06.06**

A   Professor, why is it important to keep languages alive?
B   Because the survival of languages means the preservation of cultures, too.
A   Are there many languages being lost?
B   You can see the disappearance of smaller languages all the time.
A   Can you give any examples?
B   Belorussian, the language in Belarus, hasn't died out, but it is in decline and future generations might not speak it at all.
A   What about the opposite?
B   There has been a revival in the Celtic language of Cornish.
A   But what causes language loss?
B   Basically, competition with bigger languages. The increase in English as a major international language is a massive factor. The effect goes beyond just language.
A   What do you mean?
B   Well, globalisation can also mean a deterioration in local customs.
A   That sounds depressingly true.

▶ **06.07**

1   **A** I hope you don't mind my asking, but are you around this weekend?
    B Yes, I am. Do you need a favour?
2   **A** Hi, Rosie. There's an idea I'd like to run past you.
    B What's that?
3   **A** I was wondering if you wouldn't mind helping me with something?
    B No, not at all. What is it?
4   **A** Great! I don't know how to thank you.
    B Oh, don't worry about it.
5   **A** Do you mind if I ask you to get my coat?
    B No problem, where is it?
6   **A** I'm really sorry to ask you this, but could you give me a lift home?
    B Sure, let's go.

▶ **06.08**

MARION   Good to see you, Derek! Do you mind if I ask you something?
DEREK   No, not at all. Go right ahead.
M   I hope you don't mind my asking, but I was wondering if you wouldn't mind writing a few words for the club website? We're trying to get members' profiles on there.
D   It sounds good and I'm happy to help. Just tell me what kind of thing you're looking at.
M   Super, I really appreciate it.
D   It's no trouble at all.

▶ **06.09**

1   I'm not sure people watch as much television as they used to.
2   She's also the author of a collection of children's books.
3   There are several causes of damage to our fragile environment.
4   I never got to know her niece very well, though.
5   The report suggests taking a fresh look at the health system.
6   It's an adventure story which starts with the main character in prison.
7   There was a lot of confusion and embarrassment when I put the question.
8   I do appreciate how urgent this matter has become.
9   **A** Thanks anyway for checking.
    B It's a pleasure.
10   Occasionally, I have a dessert after dinner as a treat.

▶ **06.10**

PRESENTER   Hello, and welcome to this week's travel podcast. As you know, we normally like to invite listeners in to talk about faraway places they've visited, but this week it's almost the opposite – we're talking about staycations. If you don't know what they are, well, the word 'staycation' is a combination of 'stay' and 'vacation', and it's basically a holiday that you have in your own home, or at least staying at your own home at night. Why do that? Well, for economic reasons, to avoid the stress of travelling, to explore your local area and even to enjoy your own house a little. Now, we've got three people to talk to us about their staycations. So let's speak first to Mike and hear about his … well, I won't say trip because you didn't go anywhere.

MIKE No, I didn't!

P But tell us about it anyway!

M Yes, well, I had a four-day staycation last week. I took Friday and Monday off work – my wife did too – so we had four days in all.

P And what did you do?

M Well, we'd done quite a bit of planning. So we knew there was a concert we wanted to go to on the Saturday night, and a photo exhibition as well. We also took a day trip to the coast and spent the day by the sea.

P Sounds nice.

M It was. But actually those are the things we'd do anyway, at the weekend. I think it was the little things we did differently that made the experience interesting. So, every morning, we had a big breakfast together, like in a hotel. Normally, we just eat a bowl of cereal, generally not at the same time, but this time we prepared fresh fruit, had yoghurt, something hot like mushrooms, that kind of thing. It was great to sit together and really enjoy it.

P OK.

M And also we had made some rules. No TV. No Internet. No checking emails. So we did different things – we read a lot. We listened to music, I even did some painting, and my wife wrote some poetry.

P Oh, wow. OK, now let's talk to our second guest. Samantha, tell us about your staycation.

SAMANTHA Well, I wanted it to be active, like an activity holiday. So I planned everything around that idea. I tried to do something active every day. So one day I went running in the countryside, another day I went cycling, then I went for a walk.

P Sounds tiring.

S It was, and actually on the last day, I gave up and stayed at home and slept! The other thing I did was to treat myself to a takeaway every other day. I felt I'd earned it with all that physical activity!

P Well, thanks. Now, finally, let's hear from Louise. What did you get up to?

LOUISE Well, my experience was more of a challenge because, unlike the other two, I've got two kids to entertain!

P Right, so what did you do to keep them occupied?

L Well, a bit like the others, I tried to find an activity every day. So we had a trip to the zoo, going to see a football match, going out for lunch to a restaurant, cooking all together at home, going to a concert. I tried to have the same rule as Mike – no TV or Internet – but that was too hard with kids. They couldn't understand why we'd want to change. But overall, it went quite well. I think it felt different for the kids compared to just staying at home during the school holidays. They felt we were all doing something different.

P OK, thanks, Louise. So, as usual, I'll ask you all for a mark out of ten and whether you'd recommend the holiday to our listeners. So first, Louise.

L I'd give it seven out of ten. It's not easy with kids, but it's worth a try.

P Thanks. Samantha?

S Eight out of ten. I'd recommend it, but it's probably better to have more variation instead of doing sport every single day!

P OK, and Mike?

M I really enjoyed it. You have to make an effort but if you do, I think it's a great way to spend a few days. So nine out of ten, and yes, I'd definitely recommend doing what I did.

Unit 7

▶ **07.01**

Sleep debt means you don't have enough sleep. The causes are obvious – too much work and not enough rest, basically – but what are the symptoms? Well, do you ever feel so tired in the middle of the day that you can't keep your eyes open? Do you ever get such bad headaches that you have to lie down for a while? Does this sound like you? If so, you need to do something

about it. Actually, you don't need much sleep to recover from the day, but you should make sure you get enough rest – at least seven hours each day. In fact, too much sleep, more than nine hours, can be as bad as too little sleep, six hours or less. It is a good idea to have an afternoon sleep, a siesta, especially if you can't get enough hours during the night. Some people say they feel so refreshed after a siesta that they can do twice as much. By the way, don't try not to sleep at all – people have died after too many days without sleep. Take my advice and go to bed straight away!

▶ **07.02**

There is a lot of criticism of big cities and in many ways they are soft targets. When you're driving through a major city, the traffic congestion gives you a lot of time to think, as does the time spent looking for a parking space, and you should consider the option of living in a village. There you would really need your car because public transport is almost non-existent outside major residential areas, and nearly everything, such as the kids' schools or the supermarket, would be a drive away. Let's hope you get on well with the local residents because you'll be seeing a lot of them, the same faces in the same places. Of course, with all that fresh air, the quality of life must be better, but at the same time you'll miss all the sights and sounds of the big city. It makes you think, doesn't it? So roll down your window, breathe in that air pollution and be grateful for urban development.

▶ **07.03**

Upton Abbey, the best drama series British TV has to offer, returns to your screens on Monday evening with the very first episode of Season 5. For those of you who don't know the background to *Upton Abbey*, most of the episodes are set in the UK, at the original Upton Abbey. All of that unique atmosphere of 1920s England is captured on screen with a cast of household names and a script written by the famous author, Peter Stokes. Upton Abbey is now broadcast all over the world. In fact, the first four series were recently released on many international streaming services. To make this show appropriate for all ages, some scenes were cut by our editors because they dealt with topics that not all viewers may be ready for. We want the whole family to watch! So on Monday, when you hear that familiar soundtrack come on, make sure you join us to watch the best drama on TV.

▶ **07.04**

Anne Boleyn was the second wife of Henry VIII. She was executed in 1536 to make way for Henry's new love, Jane Seymour. Anne obviously didn't take this too well and in fact there have been regular reports of people seeing Anne's ghost. Perhaps the most famous incident was at the Tower of London, where poor Anne was executed. In 1864, a soldier saw Anne and shouted at her to stop. Anne didn't and so the soldier walked right through her. The shock made him pass out.

▶ **07.05**

1 Local residents are getting worried about the crime rate.
2 There's a new shopping centre just out of town.
3 She said the living room was cosy, but really, it was just small.
4 Everyone should know the threat of climate change by now.
5 The police officers are working closely with the local community.
6 We put a solar panel on the roof to cut energy costs.
7 Disneyland is probably the best-known theme park.
8 You can never find a parking space when you need one.
9 Pour it down the kitchen sink if you don't want it.
10 More could be done to help developing nations and build a better educational system.

▶ **07.06**

JULIE Hi Sam, sorry I'm late.

SAM That's OK, Julie. Everything OK?

J Yeah, you know, just the usual – couldn't find a parking space. There just aren't enough round here.

S Yeah, I know.

J I'd have used public transport, but it probably would have taken even longer. The buses from where I work take such a long time to get into the centre. There's so much traffic congestion along the roads there.

S Yeah, I suppose I'm lucky I live so close to the centre. But sometimes I do get a bit fed up with that, to be honest.

J Really?

S Yeah, well, I think the quality of life where you live is probably better. There's so much air pollution here in the centre, and then all the traffic congestion … well, you know about that.

J Yes, I certainly do.

S Sometimes I think it would be nice to live in a big residential area like you do, instead of in the centre. In a nice detached house instead of my flat!

J Well, there are definitely advantages. I can take the underground to the centre from where I live and it's quite quick and convenient.

S Yeah, exactly.

J But there's not much for local residents, really. I mean, there are just flats and houses where I live, and a few supermarkets. No theatres, no cinemas. You've got all the entertainment you could want right on your doorstep.

S Yeah, I know – I'm lucky in a lot of ways. And if I want to get something done, it's normally quite easy – I don't have to travel too far.

J Yeah, and to be honest, I'm not sure if the air quality is much better where I live than in the centre. I mean, it's still the same city, isn't it?

S Maybe, but at least you've got a bit of greenery to help. I'm sure that sucks in some of the pollution. In the centre there's what – one park?

J Err … two.

S Oh, yeah, two. You see – I never go to the parks in the centre. They're not very nice, are they? There are people there that I don't really feel comfortable sitting next to on a bench!

J No, I agree – we've got some nice parks where I live. But you've got your terrace, haven't you? You've got some plants and flowers out there?

S Yeah, but it's not the same.

J I know, but remember what they say – the grass is always greener on the other side of the fence. You live in the centre and you dream about living where I do. And I sometimes really wish I still lived in the centre!

S Yeah?

J Of course. Just to be in the middle of everything again. But I'm sure I'd get sick of it.

S The thing is, I don't think things used to be so bad. There are so many more cars now than ten years ago. So many more people, I think.

J Yeah.

S And life just gets faster and faster. People don't know when to slow down any more. Living in the centre feels like living at double the speed of the rest of the world.

J Maybe, but it's not too different for people who commute in, you know. Everyone hurries onto the train, hurries off, hurries to the office, hurries back home.

S Yeah but in the evening, you can relax.

J Hardly. Most evenings I just think about all the work I've got to do the next day!

S Oh, it can't be that bad.

J No, I'm exaggerating. I do manage to relax in the evening.

S Me too. We should both stop complaining – I'm sure there are lots of people who'd love to live where we do.

J Agreed. Let's go and get that coffee …

Unit 8

▶ **08.01**

1 If I stop eating out, I'll save a lot of money.
2 If I didn't need to work, I'd become a full-time writer.
3 If I see Jim, I'll return the €20 I owe him.
4 If the bank didn't charge such high interest, I'd take out a bigger loan.
5 If the price is too high, I won't buy the flat.

6 If Sarah paid back her student loan any time soon, I'd be surprised.
7 If I feel generous, I might give some money to charity.
8 If I were you, I'd think about what I was doing.
9 If I worked for myself, I could have more responsibility.
10 If we spend more on advertising, profits can increase.

▶ 08.02

John Roberts made a living as a fisherman working for a big fishing company. However, John always wanted to have his own boat and business, so he put aside savings for years, and when the interest rate was low, he went to a bank. The bank checked the budget which John had prepared showing sales vs. costs and then agreed to finance the project. This meant John now had a very large debt, but he considered the boat as a sound investment. Unfortunately, business became more difficult because of overfishing and environmental damage. John's income dropped lower and lower and he was struggling just to pay off the interest on his loan. Before long the bank was starting to debit his account with penalties for missed payments. John was desperate and he wrote about his situation on a website for start-up companies. This worked. The local council immediately awarded John a grant and donations came in from people in the area. Thanks to this, John's business survived.

▶ 08.03

One night I came home very late and I couldn't find my keys, so I had to break into my own house! I was climbing through a window when a woman on the street shouted, "Police! There's a burglary!" I got down and explained that it was my house and I wasn't a burglar, but she called me a liar. She said that she was a witness and that she would give evidence when I was accused of breaking and entering. She would happily come to the trial at court to testify against me. She was really excited now and went on that the jury would find me guilty, and the judge would give me a very long prison sentence. I'd have to go to a horrible prison where the prisoners lie to one another and steal their cellmates' food just to survive. She was out of breath now and just about to start again when suddenly my house keys fell out of my back pocket. I wished her goodnight and went inside the house.

▶ 08.04

1 It should have been sent on Tuesday.
2 If I had seen her, I would have shouted.
3 If you had told me, it could have been different.
4 We'd never have known if she had stayed at home.
5 They shouldn't have thrown it away.
6 She shouldn't have taken my purse.

▶ 08.05

1 A We'll never be able to afford it.
   B Don't give up hope.
2 A I'll never see her again.
   B I'm sure you will.
3 A It started to go wrong right from the start.
   B It might work out fine.
4 A That's another opportunity lost.
   B There'll be plenty more, don't worry.
5 A I'm really worried about this interview.
   B I'm sure it'll be fine.
6 A There's not much chance of it working.
   B You never know. We might pull it off.

▶ 08.06

Really sorry to hear about your car. The same thing happened to me a couple of years ago. My car was stolen right outside my house, and believe it or not, I've just had a similar experience, I had my purse stolen from my bag when I was in the queue in the supermarket. You don't surprise me. It was just like that when I called the insurance company. They kept me waiting for ages, so I know the feeling. It was the same with me. What can you do? True, that's just like when Sarah's flat was burgled. I don't know what things are coming to.

▶ 08.07

1 Hello, this is John Peters.
2 It's Simon again from NatEast Bank.
3 It's 973 412.
4 No, but thanks anyway.
5 Do you want to pay by cash or by credit card?
6 That's fine, no worries.
7 I'm sorry, but I didn't get that.
8 All the best and speak to you soon.
9 Goodbye, thanks for calling.

▶ 08.08

PRESENTER Hello, and welcome to this week's Crime View, where we ask you for help in solving crimes in the local area. As always, you can call us on our freephone number and the information you give will go directly to the police. You don't have to leave your name, and any information you give could lead to a cash reward. So, let's turn to our first crime. Rhona Kent has the details.

RHONA Our first report is on an incident that happened at the Faylands Shopping Centre. Two weeks ago, a man walked into one of the jewellery shops here. He talked to the assistant and asked to see a number of different watches. While all this was going on, a second man entered. He appeared to look at some bracelets and other jewellery, and then he left. But soon after, staff realised that over £2,000 worth of jewellery had been taken by the second man. The men are described as being in their early thirties, both with dark hair. The second man had blue glasses.

P Thank you Rhona. Police would like to hear from anyone who has information on this. If anyone has tried to sell you jewellery on the street, in cafés and so on, please do get in touch. Now let's hear from Steven Craven about another crime the police need your help with.

STEVEN Well, in an electronics shop in Park Road three days ago, a young man was seen running out into the car park with a bag full of items taken from the shop. These items included smartphones, earbuds, tablets and a number of other expensive items. One young woman, a local student, tried to stop him after she realised that staff from the shop were shouting at him. The man accidentally knocked her over as he ran past. The woman wasn't hurt, but the thief managed to escape. The young woman said she didn't see the man's face clearly because it was too dark, but that he was wearing blue jeans and a red T-shirt.

P Thank you Steven. If you think you might know who the thief was, please get in touch. Now, we're joined in the studio by Inspector Hugh Jones, who is going to tell us about a series of crimes that have occurred over the last month or so.

INSPECTOR JONES Yes, thank you. Over the last six weeks, we've unfortunately seen thieves break into six different houses at night and steal a number of items. All these incidents have happened in quite a small area – mainly in the area between Thatch Road and Crescent Drive. It's mainly jewellery that has been stolen. In each case, the people involved were able to get in through open windows. Now, I realise that in this hot weather nobody wants to keep their windows closed, but we think that most of these crimes wouldn't have happened if the owners of the houses had taken care to close all their windows before going to bed. So please get in touch if you have any information, but also – please make sure you close your windows before going to bed, or if you're going out.

P Thank you, Inspector Jones. Now, to finish, an update on one of the crimes we featured in our previous programme. Well, police caught two men last week, accused of robbing the Newport Road petrol station back in February. They appeared in court, were found guilty and are now in prison. The names of the men involved were given directly to the police as a result of this programme. So thanks again for your help – if we hadn't received your calls, these crimes would not have been solved. So please call in with any information you might have on the stories we've covered tonight.

Unit 9

▶ 09.01

We like to think that we live in a world where everyone has access to professional medical care that can take care of their needs. Unfortunately, for those who live in the developing world, which is about 85% of the Earth's population, this is far from the case. Too often either the treatment from trained professionals which they need is impossible to get, or it costs money which they don't have. People who need treatment often then have to look for alternatives that are relatively cheap and available. There is a long tradition of using natural medicine, for example, plants whose leaves and flowers can be used to take away pain. However, natural medicine is of limited use in situations where the patient is very ill. Even so, there are people who suffer from serious diseases who trust natural medicine more than modern methods. This may sound crazy to Westerners who have the luxury of professional help, but people that believe in this kind of treatment strongly enough might benefit just from the psychological effect, which could mean the difference between life and death.

▶ 09.02

It all started when I was jogging in the park. I bumped into something, fell over and got a big bruise on my leg. It ached a bit. I was worried I had strained my leg as it wasn't comfortable. I thought it was best to do something about it, so I looked up some advice on the Internet and decided to treat myself.
There was a lot of information, all quite confusing, but I found a recipe for a special sports drink and drank a couple of litres of it. About an hour later, it hit me. I felt dizzy, my head was going round and round and I started to shiver – I couldn't hold a cup in my hands. I thought I was going to pass out, but I managed to crawl into bed. A week later, I'm beginning to get over it and thank goodness I didn't develop any complications. I won't be using any of those Internet sites again, though.

▶ 09.03

1 You've got a terrible bruise on your leg there!
2 The illness is quite serious and she needs to go to hospital.
3 The bodybuilder strained a muscle while he was working out.
4 This flu is a real nuisance – I can't do anything!
5 Eat plenty of fruit and vegetables to stay healthy.
6 I quite like my scar – I think it suits me, and it makes me look more interesting.
7 I still feel guilty for not taking care of her better.
8 May I enquire how my wife is doing, Doctor?
9 She's only had a biscuit to eat all day, so no wonder she feels dizzy.

▶ 09.04

Simon Robins was a hero when he walked around the world to raise money for charity, but journalists have now discovered that he didn't do it. Actually, Robins flew most of the way. Journalists wondered how he had done the walk so quickly and asked him to explain. At first, Robins refused to talk about it, complaining that the press wanted just to get a good story, and completely denied having anything to hide. However, journalists found out he had used a private plane and finally Robins admitted flying for part of the long journey. Robins insisted he had walked a lot of the way and promised to give money back to people who believed they had been cheated. The police have informed us that they won't be taking legal action against Robins, but they have ordered him to give a full and correct account of his 'walk' around the world.

▶ 09.05

A Hi! Do you recognise me?
B Sorry, but I've no idea who you are.
A It's Tim, from Black Street.
B Black Street? I haven't got a clue where that is.
A Oh, come on! Black Street, you must remember.
B I've really no idea. What on earth are you talking about?
A The Black Street Café. We worked there one summer.
B Oh, Tim! What on earth are you doing here?
A I wanted to ask you the same question.

A Here's your room. Have a nice stay.
B Er, I understood that we booked a large room.
A It *is* large – you should see the small rooms.
B And did I get this wrong? I thought there was a sea view.
A The sea is terrible. You don't want to see it.
B There's not even a shower!
A Have I misunderstood something? I thought you were on holiday. You'll be outside most of the time.
B But didn't you say this was a luxury hotel?
A It used to be – twenty years ago!

▶ 09.07

1 I met John in the town centre the other day.
2 Would you know where I could find a post office?
3 I can't afford it. It's too expensive.
4 That's the phone. Could you answer it, please?
5 Don't leave the window open when you go out.
6 Can you play a piece for us on the piano?
7 Don't assume I earn a lot of money from doing this.
8 There is a new trade agreement between Russia and France.
9 If it's so important to you, you can have mine.
10 I do think she ought to explain exactly what she did.

▶ 09.08

DOCTOR Good morning.
PATIENT Good morning, doctor. Excuse me.
D Take a seat. What seems to be the trouble?
P Well, it's a number of things, actually. Firstly, I think it's probably just a cold, but I wanted to check with you, really. Basically, I've got a really bad cough. And I sneeze a lot.
D Oh dear. So, how long have you had this cough?
P I'd say … I guess it's four days now. It's been worse for the last two days.
D Right.
P But I've had a few sore throats now in the last few weeks.
D And have you had a high temperature at all?
P No.
D Any aches or pains in your body?
P No.
D Well, it's probably just a cold then. Get plenty of rest, and make sure you drink lots of liquid. You'll probably get over it in a few days without having to take anything.
P OK.
D Are you taking any painkillers?
P Yes, aspirin.
D Well that's fine. That'll help the sore throat.
P What I don't understand is why I keep getting ill. This is probably the third time I've come down with a cold in the last month. It seems strange.
D Well, it can happen. There are different cold viruses and just when your body finishes fighting one, you can catch another one. It's normal at this time of year, so it's nothing to worry about.
P OK.
D But if the cough doesn't go away this time, let's say after a week, then come back and we'll give you a check to make sure you don't have a chest infection. But for now it's nothing to worry about.
P OK. Err, the other thing is that I had a bit of an accident yesterday while I was cycling.
D Yes?
P I was cycling down a hill in the forest and I don't know what happened, but I fell off. And I hurt my arm and my side, here. I've got a few bruises and it aches a bit. I just wanted to check that everything was OK.
D Right, well, er … let me just ask first – did you hit your head at all when you fell?
P A little bit, yes.
D And did you lose consciousness?
P No, no, nothing like that. I was wearing a helmet, so I just felt a bit dizzy. But I didn't feel like I was going to pass out or anything.
D Well, in any case I think you really should have gone straight to hospital to get yourself checked out if you bumped your head. Especially if you felt dizzy afterwards.
P Oh, right.

D Can I just see where you say you've got these bruises?
P Yeah, sure.
D OK … Right … Let me just feel here … Does it hurt if I do this?
P No, not really.
D OK, well yes, I think you've just got a few bruises here. Your shoulder will probably ache for a while and I think it's best if you keep off the bike for a few weeks at least.
P Oh, really? I'm supposed to be taking part in a race next week.
D Well, I wouldn't recommend that. Some gentle exercise is fine, but nothing like a race. You need to let your body get over the fall. Let me just see here … ooh, that's a very nasty cut.
P Yeah, it hurts a bit there.
D I'm going to give you a cream to treat that with. It will help it to heal and it will stop you getting any kind of infection there.
P Right.
D OK. Here you are. Put it on three times a day.
P Can I just ask one more thing?
D OK, but it will have to be very quick because I have to get on to the next patient.
P Sure. I'm going on holiday in a couple of months' time to Cambodia. I wanted to know about injections, that kind of thing.
D Right, well they can give you the information you need about that at reception. You'll need to make an appointment with one of our nurses here to get that done.
P Right.
D But speak to reception about it. They'll tell you everything you need to know.
P OK, thanks very much.
D Have a nice day.

Unit 10

▶ 10.01

Shergar was a very successful champion race horse, in fact he might have been the best ever. His racing career ended in 1981, and he could have made a lot more money for his owners from his celebrity status if he hadn't been stolen. This happened in 1983 and Shergar was never seen again.

There are lots of theories of who took Shergar and what happened to him, but in reality anything may have happened. The kidnappers must have been very professional, or very lucky, because they hid their victim so successfully. It can't have been easy to steal such a famous horse and make it disappear completely. People say the police may not have done the best job of finding the horse because they could have acted a lot more quickly – the truth is, they didn't have much evidence and the horse and its kidnappers were never found. Some people say the kidnappers must have killed Shergar when the owners didn't agree to pay the kidnappers. This must have been a tragedy for the owners and fans of Shergar. However, there may have been a happier ending. Of course, Shergar can't be alive today because this happened so many years ago. Being optimistic, he might not have been killed by the kidnappers. He could have died a natural death somewhere safe. We will probably never know.

▶ 10.02

Sally had worked as a trainee chef in a hotel for six months, but she was already dissatisfied with her job, especially the irregular hours and impolite customers. Also, Sally was still quite inexperienced, but the head chef used to get impatient with her because she couldn't do everything. Sally started to lose her self-confidence. Maybe she had unreasonable expectations? Was she just another unsuccessful trainee, and would it be dishonest to continue in a job which she couldn't do? It was highly improbable that things would get better. Sally got some informal advice from her old teacher at college, who told her to leave. For some reason – perhaps it meant she was irresponsible too – Sally didn't listen to this advice and she stayed at the hotel. This might seem incredible, but five years later, Sally is now head chef. She always smiles when her trainees tell her they want to leave.

▶ 10.03

1 The new parts are quite inexpensive.
2 I find it improbable that they just happened to be in the same place at the same time.
3 The weather at this time of the year is quite unpredictable.
4 I won't go on a trip as disorganised as this one again.
5 I've dropped it on the floor a few times, but it's unbreakable.
6 I can do it, but it's rather inconvenient, and I'm not very keen.

▶ 10.04

Shirley Chisholm (1924–2005) was the first African American woman elected to the US Congress. In 1972, she became the first African American, and the first woman, to pursue the Democratic presidential nomination.

Chisholm was born in Brooklyn, New York. At Brooklyn College, she excelled on the debate team and her professors encouraged her to try out politics. She started out teaching, but she stuck with her passion, joining organisations that tackled political and civil rights issues. In 1968, she won a seat in the US Congress. There, 'Fighting Shirley' tirelessly worked on civil rights issues. In 1972, she ran for president. She had to overcome plenty of racial discrimination; in fact, she was blocked from participating in the presidential debates, but she didn't give up – she took legal action and was allowed to give one televised speech. Although she lost the nomination, she continued in Congress until 1983. She coped with racism and sexism throughout her career, but 'Fighting Shirley' will always be remembered as a woman who fought for change.

▶ 10.05

A Hi, Lesley. Thanks for coming to see me.
B No problem, Luke. What's happened?
A I know you won't believe this, but Tim has resigned.
B Hold on. I was just speaking to Tim yesterday. He didn't say anything.
A Well, it's true. One more thing. Tim's gone to Masons.
B Hang on a minute. Masons are our competitor. That's a disaster!
A It's no tragedy. We haven't got any secrets he can tell them.
B That's true, I guess. Well, thanks for telling me. I'd better get back.
A Just a minute. There's something else we have to discuss. Would you be interested in taking Tim's job?
B What? I don't know about that. I'll have to think it over.

▶ 10.06

In the winter of eighteen fifty-five, the people of Devon in England woke up to find the footprints of a strange animal in the snow. Some frightened people followed them and the footprints went on and on … for approximately a hundred miles – if their account is to be believed. The footprints went in a straight line through gardens and over walls and roofs. No one could explain the footprints, but since then many theories have been suggested. One of the strangest was that a kangaroo had escaped from a nearby zoo and jumped through the countryside!

▶ 10.07

JOHN I don't really know how I feel it went. I was really nervous before I went in and then, when I sat down, I saw there were three people on the other side of the table! That was a bit unexpected – I thought it would just be me and one other person. Anyway, I think it went quite well – it was actually quite informal and they seemed to like me. There were a couple of questions I probably could have tackled better, but overall I really think my performance was really good.
MARTHA I really don't know what happened. I can't have left it in the café because I had it with me when I bought the newspaper at the station. And then I suppose I might have left it on the train somehow, but I don't remember ever taking it out

of my pocket. It could have fallen out, I suppose. If it did, I hope someone handed it in – it's got everything inside, cards, driving licence, you know, all those kinds of things. But I've got to admit, I don't feel very optimistic – there are so many dishonest people out there these days that you've got to think the worst, haven't you?

GENO   It was unbelievable, really – I was just walking past that clothes shop and she stopped me, said hello, and started talking about how long it had been since we'd seen each other, all that kind of thing. But I just had no idea who she was! She may have been someone I knew from school, or perhaps university. But I've got a great memory for faces and I just didn't recognise her. I think she must have confused me with someone else. Anyway, I didn't want to disappoint her, so I answered all her questions. Then we said goodbye and she went off. It was really strange!

BARRY   I think I'm very lucky. It all happened so quickly. One moment, I was going down the street, listening to my favourite radio programme, and the next thing, there was a bang and the sound of glass breaking. I suppose I must have just lost control because of the rain – it was pouring down at the time. In the end, there wasn't too much damage – there are a few repairs to do but I can still actually drive it. And the wall I hit – well, that will have to be repaired too, and I think I'll have to pay for it. But I can't complain about that – I'm just glad I'm OK because I think I could have been hurt quite badly.

EMIL   Well, one moment, we were all just talking calmly and I was trying to get everyone to agree who would do what, and then suddenly he started shouting, saying I'm always trying to pass on my work to him and that I don't work hard enough. Apart from being untrue, it was also extremely unprofessional and very impolite, shouting like that in front of everyone. I'm really furious now – I mean, who does he think he is, behaving like that? It's not the first time he's lost his temper like that with someone, so it wasn't like a big surprise. I know he has a lot of problems, and I suppose he might have had a really difficult day or something. But we're all under stress, aren't we? I'm going to have to make a formal complaint about him, I think.

Acknowledgements

The authors and publishers acknowledge the following sources of copyright material and are grateful for the permissions granted. While every effort has been made, it has not always been possible to identify the sources of all the material used, or to trace all copyright holders. If any omissions are brought to our notice, we will be happy to include the appropriate acknowledgements on reprinting and in the next update to the digital edition, as applicable.

Key:
U = Unit.

Photographs
The following photographs are sourced from Getty Images.
U1: FatCamera/E+; Asurobson/iStock/Getty Images Plus; Chef2323@hotmail.co.uk kevin/iStock Editorial/Getty Images Plus; Avid_creative/E+; AndreyPopov/iStock/Getty Images Plus; BWFolsom/iStock/Getty Images Plus; Marcus Lindstrom/E+; DrGrounds/E+; Jordan Siemens/Stone; Jason LaVeris/FilmMagic; Maskot; **U2:** Colin Langford/500px; Rachel Lewis/Lonely Planet Images/Getty Images Plus; Kentaroo Tryman/Maskot; MR1805/iStock/Getty Images Plus; SanerG/iStock/Getty Images Plus; Ali Trisno Pranoto/Moment; Freder/E+; **U3:** PeopleImages/E+; YinYang/iStock/Getty Images Plus; Mike Powell/Getty Images Sport; JEFF HAYNES/AFP; JGI/Jamie Grill; **U4:** Moment RF collection; Zero Creatives/Cultura; FRANCOIS XAVIER MARIT/AFP; Frédéric Soltan/Corbis News; Kali9/E+; **U5:** Grant Dixon/Lonely Planet Images/Getty Images Plus; Ray Hems/E+; Kasipat Phonlamai/EyeEm; Schmidt-z/E+; Marco Bottigelli/Moment; AdrianHancu/iStock/Getty Images Plus; Roger Coulam/Oxford Scientific/Getty Images Plus; Rob Atherton/iStock Editorial/Getty Images Plus; Kanvag/iStock/Getty Images Plus; Ian.CuiYi/Moment; MarioGuti/iStock Unreleased; SAUL LOEB/AFP; Tassii/E+; **U6:** Renato Vieira Da Silva/EyeEm; Philippe Roy/Cultura; Monkeybusinessimages/iStock/Getty Images Plus; ArxOnt/Moment; F11photo/iStock/Getty Images Plus; Photos.com/Getty Images Plus; Kali9/E+; **U7:** Kritchanut/iStock/Getty Images Plus; Westend61; SDI Productions/E+; Milan2099/E+; Nikada/iStock/Getty Images Plus; **U8:** Taylanibrahim/iStock/Getty Images Plus; Webphotographeer/E+; Westend61; BrAt_PiKaChU/iStock/Getty Images Plus; Cavan Images; Pawel.gaul/E+; **U9:** Hiraman/E+; Andresr/E+; Mlenny/E+; Filadendron/E+; Cscredon/E+; Andersen Ross/DigitalVision; **U10:** Winhorse/E+; Andresr/E+; Bettmann; Cecilie_Arcurs/E+; Borchee/E+; FluxFactory/iStock/Getty Images Plus; Thomas Barwick/DigitalVision; Ariel Skelley/DigitalVision.

The following photographs are sourced from other libraries.

U5: Ollyy/Shutterstock; **U7:** David R. Frazier Photolibrary, Inc./Alamy Stock Photo.

Cover Photography by Stanislaw Pytel/Stone/Getty Images.

Illustrations
QBS Learning; Mark Bird; Sean/KJA; Greg Roberts; David Semple; Vicky Woodgate.

Video stills
Commissioned by Rob Maidment and Sharp Focus Productions.

Filming in King's College by kind permission of the Provost and Scholars of King's College, Cambridge.

Audio production by Hart McLeod and by Creative Listening.

Typeset by QBS Learning.

Corpus
Development of this publication has made use of the Cambridge English Corpus (CEC). The CEC is a computer database of contemporary spoken and written English, which currently stands at over one billion words. It includes British English, American English, and other varieties of English. It also includes the Cambridge Learner Corpus, developed in collaboration with the University of Cambridge ESOL Examinations. Cambridge University Press has built up the CEC to provide evidence about language use that helps us to produce better language teaching materials.

English Profile
This product is informed by English Vocabulary Profile, built as part of English Profile, a collaborative program designed to enhance the learning, teaching, and assessment of English worldwide. Its main funding partners are Cambridge University Press and Cambridge Assessment English and its aim is to create a 'profile' for English, linked to the Common European Framework of Reference for Languages (CEFR). English Profile outcomes, such as the English Vocabulary Profile, will provide detailed information about the language that learners can be expected to demonstrate at each CEFR level, offering a clear benchmark for learners' proficiency. For more information, please visit www.englishprofile.org.

CALD
The Cambridge Advanced Learner's Dictionary is the world's most widely used dictionary for learners of English. Including all the words and phrases that learners are likely to come across, it also has easy-to-understand definitions and example sentences to show how the word is used in context. The Cambridge Advanced Learner's Dictionary is available online at dictionary.cambridge.org.

Shaftesbury Road, Cambridge CB2 8EA, United Kingdom

One Liberty Plaza, 20th Floor, New York, NY 10006, USA

477 Williamstown Road, Port Melbourne, VIC 3207, Australia

314–321, 3rd Floor, Plot 3, Splendor Forum, Jasola District Centre, New Delhi – 110025, India

103 Penang Road, #05–06/07, Visioncrest Commercial, Singapore 238467

Cambridge University Press & Assessment is a department of the University of Cambridge.

We share the University's mission to contribute to society through the pursuit of education, learning and research at the highest international levels of excellence.

www.cambridge.org
Information on this title: www.cambridge.org/9781108961363

© Cambridge University Press & Assessment 2022

First published 2022

20 19 18 17 16 15 14 13 12 11 10 9 8 7 6 5

Printed in Malaysia by Vivar Printing

A catalogue record for this publication is available from the British Library

ISBN 978-1-108-95808-0 Upper Intermediate Student's Book with eBook
ISBN 978-1-108-96131-8 Upper Intermediate Student's Book with Digital Pack
ISBN 978-1-108-96135-6 Upper Intermediate Workbook with Answers
ISBN 978-1-108-96136-3 Upper Intermediate Workbook without Answers
ISBN 978-1-108-96133-2 Upper Intermediate Combo A with Digital Pack
ISBN 978-1-108-96134-9 Upper Intermediate Combo B with Digital Pack
ISBN 978-1-108-96137-0 Upper Intermediate Teacher's Book with Digital Pack
ISBN 978-1-108-95951-3 Upper Intermediate Presentation Plus
ISBN 978-1-108-96132-5 Upper Intermediate Student's Book with Digital Pack,
Academic Skills and Reading Plus

Additional resources for this publication at cambridge.org/empower

This page is intentionally left blank.